# DOING AFRICAN CHRISTIAN THEOLOGY:

## An Evangelical Perspective

**Richard J. Gehman**

# DOING AFRICAN CHRISTIAN THEOLOGY:
## An Evangelical Perspective

ISBN 9966-850-13-9

*Printed and Published by*
**Evangel Publishing House**
**P.O. Box 28963,**
**Nairobi**

PRINT No. 10 9 8 7 6 5 4 3 2 1

# INTRODUCTION

These are exciting days for the Church of Jesus Christ in Africa. Churches are growing more rapidly than ever before.

Whereas, there were only 9,900,000 professing Christians in Africa in 1900, David Barrett projects a total of 393,000,000 people professing Christ by the year 2,000 (Barrett 1982). Never before in the history of the Christian Church has a whole continent turned to Christianity within one century. The vast percentage of the populations of many countries will be Christian within another decade. About 84% of Uganda, 83% of Zambia and 82% of Kenya are projected to embrace Christianity by the year A.D. 2,000.

Part of church growth in Africa is in the dimension of theological maturity. Until recent years, the theology taught this younger church was largely imported from overseas, reflecting the Christian thought of Americans and Europeans rooted in their cultural past. In these days African theologians are rising in their quest to make their Christian faith authentically an African Christian faith. John Mbiti, a leading African theologian, has declared:

> Christianity has made a real claim on Africa...the question is: Has Africa made a real claim on Christianity? Christianity has Christianized Africa, but Africa has not africanized Christianity. (McGavran 1972:144)

We live in a new day. The foundation of the Christian Church in Africa has been laid. The peoples of this great continent are being called out to become "a chosen race" and "a holy nation" in order to proclaim the glory of God (I Pet. 2:9).

Furthermore, the African Christian Church has come of age in that she is now providing her administrative and teaching leadership to chart her future under the guidance of the Holy Spirit. African theologians are rising and seeking ways to relate the Gospel to their context by addressing those particular problems which African Christians face. As the African Church studies the Scriptures and discerns God's will, she will become less dependent upon others with alien perspectives.

This book on **Doing African Christian Theology: An Evangelical Perspective** is intended as a survey of the origins of theology in Africa, an evaluation of the basic methodological approach of African Christian Theology, and a proposal for the African evangelical church to develop her own African Christian Theology.

The basic purpose of this book is twofold: to alert the evangelicals concerning the faulty foundations for some of African Christian Theology; and to challenge the evangelicals to become engaged in this necessary task of reflecting on God's revelation of Himself and His will for His people in the context of Africa.

The perspective of this book is decidedly evangelical in nature. Like so many words, "evangelical" means many things to different people. In some countries of the world an evangelical is another name for Protestant. The Protestant Reformation of the 16th century was indeed evangelical to the core. They stressed the "good news" of Jesus Christ with salvation from sin by grace through faith alone. But with the advent of rationalism entering the Protestant Churches, liberalism gradually rejected or reinterpreted the historic Christian doctrines.

Therefore, we use the term, evangelical, to denote that theological perspective which affirms the basic biblical doctrines of the Christian Church, such as: the Trinity, the deity of Christ, the personality of the Holy Spirit, the substitutionary death of Christ as an atonement for the sins of His people, Christ's bodily resurrection from the grave, His ascension into heaven, His personal and visible return again, the resurrection and judgment of all men, the final state of all men and women either in heaven or hell. Basic to all evangelical thinking is the plenary and verbal inspiration of the Holy Scriptures so that they are without error in all that they teach.

Since the author is a member of the Africa Inland Mission and serving in the Africa Inland Church of Kenya for the past twenty years, he has done some research within his circles of fellowship. However, what is said most naturally applies to most African Christian churches for most of the Protestant founding missions were fervently evangelical in their roots. Indeed, even today the grass roots of most African Protestant Christian churches reflect those evangelical origins. Only with the advent of liberalism penetrating the theological training of African leaders, both in Africa and overseas, has the evangelical foundation begun to crumble.

The intention in this book is both negative and positive. On the negative side, evangelicals must be alerted to the theological trends in Africa which are based on a faulty view of Scripture. But on the positive side, evangelicals must be challenged to fulfill their God given responsibility. Not only must the lost be evangelized, both outside and inside the churches, but the people of God must grow in their obedience to Jesus Christ as they reflect upon God's revealed will in their particular context of life. Unless evangelicals search the Scriptures for themselves and seek to gain a knowledge of God's will for various issues that face them, they will fall into disobedience. And unless evangelicals become more and more a people of the Book, they shall loose their evangelical fervency. Revival and renewal in the churches depend upon a prayerful meditation upon the Word of God.

As evangelicals let us take the challenge of John Mbiti. Let us think through our Christian faith in our African context, but always under the authority of the Word of God. Let us seek to be genuinely and thoroughly African in our Christian Theology, and absolutely biblical in our conclusions.

# CONTENTS

Artwork by Darwin Dunham

# *Chapter 1*

# *THE NEED*

## PERSONAL REFLECTIONS

The need for African Christian Theology has gradually been impressed upon the author over the years. A couple of personal experiences may help us to understand this need.

Although I was reared in a Christian home and was converted at a young age, Christ did not seem very near to me. Somehow the person of Jesus Christ was distant. In contrast, God as Spirit was real to me. I loved Him, read His Word faithfully, obeyed Him and tried to serve Him. As I grew older I became aware that Christ, the Word of God made flesh, manifested in human flesh the true nature of God to mankind. Why was it that God as Spirit I loved, but Christ, God manifest in the flesh, seemed to be more distant to me?

After years of reflection on my personal experience I concluded that this was due to the image I had of Jesus Christ. His long hair and bearded face simply did not attract me to Him. Whenever I thought of Jesus Christ I thought of those portraits of Jesus Christ with a full beard and shoulder length hair. That simply was not the image of One I could love.

Now as a matter of historical fact Jesus Christ probably did wear long hair with a beard. If we desire historical accuracy, then our image of Jesus Christ incarnate should include a bearded face. But what of those cultural experiences we have had which shape our ideal of what is valuable and good? Some of our cultural values may fall short of God's glory and we will need to adjust our traditional values to conform to God's standards. But in the communication of the Gospel we need to be oriented to the cultural heritage of the receivers if we are to communicate most effectively. To this day I find it advantageous to imagine Christ clean faced and with "properly cut hair." This may reflect my age or my own cultural background. But whatever it may disclose, the facts are that shoulder length hair and a full bearded face do not appeal to me even today.

This has cross cultural implications. Whenever the Gospel is communicated cross culturally, there must be a real measure of identification with the peoples. Christ must be presented in a manner that is both true to Scripture and meaningful to the people. True, Jesus Christ is Lord of all. But He is also Lord of each given

1

people group. Christ must be seen and known and understood in the context of each culture. Even as God, the Eternal Spirit, became incarnate as a human being in a particular culture, so Jesus Christ must belong to each society in a unique way.

Back in 1967, one year after arriving in Kenya as a missionary, my wife and I visited a church in Fort Hall (Muranga, today) decorated with remarkable Goya-like mural paintings by a Chagga artist called Elimo Njau. They depict the birth of Christ, His ministry and crucifixion. But Christ is an African, Mary and Joseph are Africans, and all the scenes are painted with an African landscape. My initial reaction was one of rejection, for the message communicated was contrary to the facts. Jesus, the son of David, the son of Abraham, was a Jew. And Jews histori-cally are not black. The scene of Jesus' birth was in Palestine, not in Africa.

Technically, that is all true. Yet over the years I have come to appreciate the dynamics which went into the painting of those murals. And my own experience with the image of Jesus confirmed that. Furthermore, I realized that the usual portraits of Jesus used in the West, such as Sallman's Head of Christ, are not truly reflective of Jesus either. For Christ was from Palestine, a Middle Easterner with darker skin. But Sallman's Head of Christ portrays Jesus more as an Anglo Saxon with facial features and facial colour more representative of a West European than a Jew from the Middle East.

We are confronted with two important issues: truth and meaning. Evangeli-cals have long been emphatic on maintaining the truth of the Gospel as revealed in Scripture. In our personal reflections we have observed that the facts are one thing. Jesus Christ, God incarnate in human flesh, was not an African. Nor was He a European. We must seek to understand something of Jesus' personal ap-pearance through historical research.

But the truth of the Gospel must be applied to each person in his own culture. Christ must be understood and welcomed in culturally relevant ways. What does the Gospel mean to me? In one sense we are continually driven back to the Scrip-tures to answer that question. Even the meaning of the truth ultimately is deter-mined by the inscripturated Word of God. But we all live existentially with pecul-iar experiences, problems and needs. And so that truth with many and varied facets is applied to our own lives in a meaningful way, partly governed by our cul-tural context, but hopefully, as believers, through the guidance of the Holy Spirit.

There is great need to interpret Jesus Christ to the African in such a way that we are both true to the Scriptures and meaningful to the African. Every believer must be made to feel at home with his Christian faith. This will necessitate a con-siderable measure of assimilation of traditional African culture into the expres-sion of the Christian faith. Wherever an African tradition can be purified and re-tained for the glory of God, this should be done in African Christianity so that the Christian faith will have genuine marks of African indigeneity.

## UNIVERSAL TRUTH OF THE GOSPEL

As evangelicals we believe in the relevancy of Jesus Christ and His Gospel for all peoples. God is the Creator of all men and women. We were all made in the image of God. We are all sons and daughters of Adam and Eve. And through Adam we have all fallen into sin. Our basic needs are all the same. The Gospel by its very nature is relevant for all people.

The initial reaction of people who visit other cultures is shock over the differences. How different we behave. How different we live. And how frustratingly different are our values. These differences are the stuff of anthropology and the reason missionaries need training in cross cultural ministry.

But emphasis on differences can be over done, even though I still admit to occasional frustration over the problems of communication that arise in ministry among peoples of a different culture. The facts are that people as human beings are very much the same. We have the same physical, social, psychological and spiritual needs. And we have the same potential for growth and development. We all need the Good News concerning Jesus Christ, the Saviour of the world, as taught in the Bible

Theologically, we base our confidence in the universal truth and universal relevancy of the Gospel on the nature of God and man.

The only true and living God created man and woman in His own image for the purpose of communication and fellowship (Gen. 1:26-28). True, God is holy but He is not Wholly Other. While God in His essence is separate from the creatures, He has created mankind with His own image stamped on them. Thus men and women have the potential of being more like God than like the animal kingdom. They were created to glorify God through their mind, will and emotions. Fellowship between God and His creatures made in His image is potentially possible. Whereas, there is no such possibility of fellowship with the animal kingdom. In brief, God created men and women in order for God to communicate His will to us and for us to glorify God through faith and obedience.

Because of sin God has communicated His love and message of redemption through the Old Testament prophets and in these last days God has spoken through His Son, Jesus Christ (Heb. 1:1). The Bible is God's inspired revelation of this Good News of salvation. And this divine revelation is intended for everyone.

The Gospel of Jesus Christ as defined by Holy Scriptures belongs to every person in every culture under the sun. On the one hand, when Jesus Christ became man, He of necessity had to become a particular man in a particular culture. In this sense He is a foreigner to most peoples - a Jew from a tiny middle eastern country, born 2,000 years ago. On the other hand, the locality of Jesus' birth and ministry is symbolic of the great truth that He belongs to every race, culture and language.

Palestine, the place of birth and ministry of Jesus, is on a land bridge connecting the three continents where all the ancient civilizations were located. Jesus was not born in Europe. Paul the missionary carried the Gospel to Greece and Rome from its home base in Antioch. Lydia became the first European Christian on Paul's second missionary journey (Acts 16:14). Jesus was not born in Asia. He was born in the Middle East. Nor was Jesus an African, though His home was so close to Africa that He found refuge with Mary and Joseph in Egypt when Herod the Great, the king of the Jews, sought to kill Jesus (Mt. 2:13ff).

Truly, in the providence of God the very place of Jesus' birth and ministry is parabolic of the fact that Jesus Christ and His Gospel belongs to the whole human race. Nor is there one race or nation or language which is closer to His heart of love than any other.

By the grace of God He has established One Holy Catholic Church built upon Christ Jesus the cornerstone. Everyone who is saved by grace through faith in Jesus Christ is a member of Christ's Church which is His Body (Eph. 2:1-22). The word, "catholic," simply means "universal." The true Church is not identified with any visible organization in this world. Wherever men and women place their faith in Jesus Christ to save them from their sins, they have become a member of the One Holy Catholic Church which is found throughout the world today. Those who were once strangers to one another, even traditional enemies, have become united in One Body with Jesus Christ as the Head (Eph. 4:4-6).

As men and women, born by the Spirit of God (Jn. 3:3-8), we are united in "one faith" (Eph. 4:5). God has given to all believers the One Holy Spirit (Jn. 14:25-26; 15:26-27; 16:12-14). And He has given to His Church various gifts, including pastors and teachers, to equip the saints so that we might grow up in the Body of Christ, "until we all attain to the unity of the faith." (Eph. 4:7-13)

The emphasis in Scriptures is on the "unity of faith." God has one Gospel centring in One Saviour to be communicated to all peoples. The Bible, though written in different cultures by many men, from the Patriarch Moses to the Apostle John, spanning nearly 1,600 years, is yet marked by complete unity due to the superintending work of the Holy Spirit. "No prophecy was ever made by an act of human will, but men moved by the Holy Spirit spoke from God." (II Pet. 1:21) Thus the Bible contains all that God has wanted to communicate to mankind, and only what He wants to communicate.

We might compare the great diversity of human cultures with the bewildering array of Christian denominations. Beneath the amazing differences among people and their cultures, there is a unity. This unity is found within the people themselves who are more alike than their cultures because we all have one father and mother.

Even so in Christianity there is a bewildering range of denominations, stressing one thing or another. The Bible does not speak of a multitude of denominations but it does speak of One Body of Christ. The Bible does not make distinctions between differing denominations but it does distinguish between those who are saved and those who are not; between those who are dead in trespasses and sins and those who have been raised to a new life in Christ; between those who are children of God through faith in Christ and those who are children of the devil because of unbelief.

4

Born again believers are more alike throughout the world than their bewildering array of denominations might suggest because God is their Father by the Holy Spirit and Jesus Christ is their One Lord. Thus when we go beneath the wide range of Christian beliefs and practices found in the various denominations and learn to know the professing Christians themselves, we soon discover whether they know Jesus Christ personally or not. Those who truly know God through a personal faith in Christ are knit together with ourselves despite the denominational differences. We love the Lord Jesus Christ together, we pray together, we witness together before others of our one faith in Christ who has died for our sins and can change their lives even as He as done ours. We are one in Christ.

God's purpose for us as brothers and sisters in Christ is to study the Scriptures together to know His will for our lives. Herein is the shame of our divisions. Instead of sharing together in prayer and Bible study, we separate ourselves into contending groups, arguing and contending with each other. What we ought to do as brothers and sisters who disagree on our understanding of some biblical teaching is to seek God's will through mutual study of the Bible and in mutual love.

God has given us His revelation in the Bible. Since God is the Author (II Tim. 3:16,17), there is unity throughout the Scriptures, from Genesis to Revelation. Though different perspectives are found, reflecting different cultural backgrounds and personal experiences of the human authors, there is ultimate unity because the Holy Spirit is the One Divine Author.

We conclude, then, that God is One and that He has given the one Gospel to all men. As members of the One Body of Jesus Christ we earnestly seek God's will from His divine revelation, the Bible. In Scripture we find universal truth intended for all of God's people. Our responsibility is to develop and grow in our understanding, having our minds continually renewed by the Holy Spirit through the study of the Bible.

## LOCAL CONTEXT OF THE GOSPEL

We have briefly sketched the universality of the Gospel and its relevancy for all peoples. Our main concern, however, is to demonstrate that we need to apply and relate that Gospel to each context where people embrace Christ as Lord and Saviour. Each society understands the Word of God through their coloured glasses of a particular culture and historical context.

In the past, cross cultural missionaries had sought to relate the teaching of the Bible to the local cultures. This was known as "indigenization." "Indigenous" is derived from Latin and means, "to bear or produce within." The intended idea was that Christianity must become "native," that is, "born, growing or produced within." Until Christianity is planted indigenously, until the Christian Church takes on the colouring of a given culture, Christianity remains foreign.

Missionary theory in the past generations included the idea of planting indigenous churches. This was summarized by the three "selfs": self governing, self propagating and self supporting. The goal of the missionary endeavour was to plant churches which could multiply themselves within their own culture without

5

the need for dependence upon foreign finance or personnel. Indigenization also included the utilization of traditional culture for the communication of the Gospel. The intention of this teaching on indigenization was autonomy and self-reliance of churches in every given culture instead of dependence upon the missionary sending churches.

The term, "contextualization," has come into popular use in the past decade, supplanting the traditional use of the word, "indigenization." Shoki Coe and Aharon Sapsezian, directors of the "Theological Education Fund" (TEF), first used the word in 1972 with the publication of TEF's Third Mandate, entitled, **Ministry in Context.** Simply stated, contextualization is "the capacity to respond meaningfully to the Gospel within the framework of one's situation." (Coe 1972)

As presented by Shoki Coe and the Theological Education Fund Third Mandate, contextualization is not something radically different. It embraces everything which was meant by indigenization. Yet it is concerned with changing societies in the modern 20th century so that the Gospel is made relevant to modern day issues of justice, liberation, non-Christian religions, and economic power. Thus contextualization is concerned with the dynamic, changing context of present day culture, and not merely with an imagined static, traditional culture.

Because of the liberal theological perspective of many scholars who advocate contextualization, various evangelicals have tried to avoid the use of the term. James Buswell rightly contended that "indigenization" is perfectly capable of bearing this enlarged meaning (Buswell 1978a:17). After Bruce Fleming traced the historical development of contextualization with all "the implied theology," he advocates another expression, "context-indigenizing." (Fleming 1980)

Words can mean whatever we intend them to mean. Furthermore, the original definition given to contextualization by Shoki Coe and the TEF is perfectly acceptable to evangelicals: "the capacity of responding meaningfully to the Gospel within the framework of one's own situation." Therefore, we shall speak of contextualization with that definition in mind and with an implied evangelical theology.

As evangelicals we accept the Truth of God's revelation in the Bible. That Truth is of universal relevance. Wherever God communicates that Truth, peoples in their various cultures are compelled to make a decision: either believe and obey and thereby be changed, or to reject and disobey and thereby remain under the judgment of God.

But we also recognize that divine revelation becomes meaningful in different ways to different peoples under different situations. As a child I grew up in a rather sheltered Christian atmosphere. Having been saved at the tender age of five and having been preserved from gross sin by God's grace, I never really had a moving experience of conversion from sin. In my own experience the truth of God which bore deeply into my soul was the providential grace of God in calling me to His service and leading me step by step into the ministry.

I can recall vividly over the years a certain measure of distress that the redemption of Christ from sin was not as meaningful to me as it ought to have been, so it seemed to me. God's presence was real. His sovereign control over my life was beyond dispute. With profound awareness I knew that God had separated me from my mother's womb to be His child and to serve Him in Africa. There was no doubt. As a teenager I was reading the Scriptures and came across the words of the prophet, Isaiah. "The Spirit of the Lord God is upon me, Because the Lord has anointed me to bring good news to the afflicted..." (Isa. 61:1) Never before had I seen that verse but it expressed exactly what my experience had been. I knew that the Spirit of God was upon me and anointing me to preach the Good News. Consequently, I wrote in my Bible, "my life's verse." And so it has been ever since.

It was not until years later that God began to work in my own life, disclosing the utter sinfulness of my own heart before Him. These were not public sins, known and seen by all. But they were horrible sins before a holy God. Only as an adult believer, years after my new birth, did I become more and more conscious of the grace of Jesus Christ in my own life. Years after God had profoundly disclosed Himself as my Lord did He begin to reveal Himself as the gracious Saviour whose death on the cross was essential for my salvation.

Theologically, one might insist that the order should have been reversed. Should not I have been gripped by the grace of God in my salvation before moving on to a deeper understanding of God's will for my life? Logically, that may be true. But God is not restricted by our logic. He meets us where we are. He speaks to us where we currently need Him.

Contextualization is "the capacity to respond meaningfully to the Gospel within the framework of one's own situation..." Not only is the Gospel true, it has profound meaning to us. And various parts of the Word of God have special meaning to different people in differing contexts.

Both truth and meaning of God's Word are essential. "All Scripture is inspired by God and profitable..." (11 Tim. 3:16) Hereby is usually the distortion of the truth, the unbalanced emphasis of one Scripture while ignoring another counterbalancing truth. Therefore, as Christians we are obligated to return again and again to Scripture to learn from God all that He has said to us, for all of it is profitable.

Nevertheless, in our finite existence we are incapable of understanding and appropriating all of the truth of Scripture at once. We must learn line upon line, precept upon precept. And God usually speaks to us where we are- in our given historical and cultural context. Scripture becomes meaningful to us as the truth of God's Word interfaces with our own experiences. A child in first grade is hardly interested in those experiences of a university student. A man in Brazil is seldom interested in the experiences of a woman in Egypt. In like manner God has a meaningful word to speak to each child of God in his own given context. And that word is meaningful, not only because it is God's Word but because of the context in which he finds himself.

# HISTORICAL NEED FOR AFRICAN CHRISTIAN THEOLOGY

There is real need today for the Body of Christ in Africa which is the Church of Jesus to think through various cultural questions in the light of the Word of God. All believers everywhere struggle with problems which need resolution through theological reflection on the Scriptures. The problems we face in Africa are unique, owing to the unique circumstances in which we find ourselves. By the grace of God and through the course of time a growing number of mature, educated African believers are being produced in the churches who are able to study the Scriptures in the light of their context. They are able in consultation with all believers to arrive at a consensus as to what God is saying to His people in this particular context.

What a contrast to years gone by when theological beliefs were simply taught them by missionaries. Theological reflection was done by missionaries along with national believers. But the colonial context did not provide that encouragement to allow the Christian nationals to arrive at their own conclusions. Whatever involvement there was by the African believers, and they were definitely involved, the final decisions were often made by the missionaries.

A few historical examples may help us to understand the historical background from which we have come and point the way to our present urgent need for theological reflection by evangelical African believers.

## United Missionary Approach

In Kenya the four main Protestant missions which pioneered Christian witness from the beginning were the Church Missionary Society, Church of Scotland Mission, the Africa Inland Mission and the United Methodist Mission. Though they came from various national and denominational backgrounds, they were united in their evangelical faith. Between 1909 and 1932 five Missionary Conferences were held, dealing with issues of mutual interest, such as comity, mutual relations of the missions and the establishment of a United African Church. In the 1909 United Missionary Conference, Archdeacon Willis of the C.M.S. read a paper entitled, "The Desirability of a Single Native Church in British East Africa." (Cole 1957)

By the time of the United Missionary Conference held at Kikuyu in 1913 there was a growing consensus that the Christian witness in British East Africa should be a united witness. Charles Hurlburt, Director of the A.I.M., had gone on record that the A.I.M. believed that "the church of the future should be on Church of England lines." (Cope 1979:100)

Arising out of the Kikuyu conference of 1913, a Continuation Committee drew up proposals for an Alliance of Missionary Societies in British East African Protectorate. Their ultimate goal was a "United African Church within the Protectorate" for the purpose of presenting a visible unity among the Christians (C.C.K.C. 1918).

Because such a Church Union was thought to be premature at that moment, an Alliance of Mission Societies was formed in order to prepare the way for an eventual United African Church. Therefore, the Church Missionary Society, the Church of Scotland Mission, the Africa Inland Mission and the Methodists agreed to do everything possible to prepare for this eventual union. They developed the local church organizations along similar lines, sought to establish similar standards of discipline among the church members, respected the status of every Christian assigned to him by the branch of the Church of Christ to which he belonged, and sought to prepare the believers for eventual union (C.C.K.C.1918).

The United African Church never was achieved. The first obstacle was the objection of the Anglo Catholics within the Anglican Church (Cole 1957:5). The concluding problem was the development of liberalism within several of the missions which alienated the A.I.M. from such a merger (A.M.S. 1922). Nevertheless, for many years there was consultation and agreement among the Protestant Missions as to their approach to various cultural problems faced by them.

This attempt to form a united Christian Church in Kenya by evangelicals played an important part in the united stand of the Protestant missions toward questions of African culture. Because these missionaries were all evangelical in their theology and because they were working together to present the Gospel with singular appeal, these missionaries tried to approach questions of African culture with one accord.

## Participation of Nationals

To suggest that the missionaries made their conclusions by themselves without consultation with the African believers is to distort the historical facts. From the beginning there was in fact discussion and consultation between the expatriate missionaries and the national believers.

An example can be given from the Church of Scotland Mission. While the C.M.S. tolerated drinking of alcoholic beverages, the C.S.M. and A.I.M. advocated total abstinence. John W. Arthur, missionary leader of the Church of Scotland Mission, reported that both the missionaries and their Gikuyu Christians, advocated total abstinence. After a two year experiment in which Africans were prevented from entering into the catechumenate if they refused to take a vow of total abstinence from alcoholic liquor, the young male Gikuyu Christians pressed Arthur to call a meeting to thrash out the question.

> At our Church meeting on Saturday, the question was raised and fought out. It was entirely a native **shauri** and a straight fight between the young men, who were all on, not on only not to drink, but to forbid it in the buying of their girls etc., and two or three of the older Christians who made the opposition...
>
> In the end there were two plain issues:- 1) That drinking or tasting of beer by Christians be prohibited. Only two or three of the older ones admitted to still taking it. The motion carried with only one discontent, 55 full Church members voting for it. 2)That beer in payment of buying a girl, or for work done, should also be prohibited. (Arthur n.d.)

9

One of the older Christians stated in the meeting that if the missionaries had ordered prohibition, he would have refused to obey. But since the "Native Church" desired it, he was willing to agree.

In another Conference of Kikuyu Church Elders, May 8-12,1929, they all agreed that beer was evil and should be forbidden in all churches, and made a matter of discipline (C.K.E. 1929).

Not only were African believers given a decisive voice in many decisions of church practice, they themselves were the ones who frequently decided to give up many of the African customs. Various missionaries themselves contend that they did not force African believers to surrender their cultural practices, but that this was the choice of African Christians.

Linnell Davis, a missionary with the Africa Inland Mission and born in Kenya of missionary parents near the turn of the century, interviewed various older Christians and asked them why they took a particular approach to the Akamba cultural traditions. "Did the missionaries put this in your mind?" he asked them. In almost every case they said that the more they studied the Scriptures, they came to their own conclusion.

In fact the A.I.M. missionaries in Ukambani had made the decision that any ruling about customs should be left up to the mature African Christians. They felt that the people had to decide for themselves. The fact that the African Christians had made the decision regarding their customs, ensured that the decision would be long lasting. No missionary could impose his will on the people with lasting results (Davis 1982:P.I).

The caricature of the older missionary these days is that of one who robbed the African of his culture and imposed the European culture on him. Mrs. Guilding, an A.I.M. missionary among the Akamba during the early part of the century, contends that the A.I.M in Ukambani did not place pressure on the Africans to change their own culture. The missionaries felt their own responsibility was to teach the Bible but not to force change. For instance, the A.I.M missionaries in Ukambani never legislated against female circumcision (Guilding n.d.: T.I.). Martha Davis, wife of Linnell Davis and long time missionary among the Akamba, affirmed that this is what she always had heard from the older missionaries. While the missionaries felt a responsibility to teach the Bible and advise, they placed no pressure on them to change (Davis 1982:P.I.).

In fact an example can be given of missionaries forbidding the Africans to adapt European ways. Many early A.I.M. missionaries in Ukambani discouraged the wearing of European clothes, parting of hair and learning of English. They stressed the Kikamba Bible. Linnell Davis remembers a time when an African came into the church with shoes on and for this reason C.F. Johnston sent him out of the church (Davis 1982:P.I). While this undoubtedly was paternalism, it does reflect the desire of the missionaries not to encourage or even tolerate European enculturation.

The Akamba in fact resented Johnston's approach to European clothes and the learning of English. A case can be made for the belief that the Africans desired

10

to emulate the missionary in his dress, behaviour and life style. When Mrs. Elwood Davis, mother of Linnell Davis, arrived in Machakos in 1911, she sensed the African resentment and therefore, began helping the women to sew their own dresses. She became renowned in Ukambani and greatly appreciated for this (Davis 1982:P.I.).

Eric Barnett, another A.I.M second generation missionary, maintains that in his experience the missionaries did not seek to change anything in the African culture except that which African Christians themselves said was evil. Nothing was said of dress or the food they ate. The Africans chose to wear the European clothes. Charms used to ward off evil spirits were removed. But almost always it was the African who forbad it (Barnett 1982:P.I).

Linnell Davis insists that it was the African which took the strict stand against polygamy. Some missionaries were more lenient. "In my knowledge," says Rev. Davis, "African church leaders tried to arrange for the men to give up all their wives except their first one, but only in a suitable way, so that the wives had houses provided for them and with an income to support them, or through marrying another man." (Davis 1982:P.I.)

Jean Baxter who arrived at Kapsabet among the Nandi as an A.I.M. missionary in 1936 speaks of the advice given her by Stuart Bryson, the senior A.I.M missionary. "Speak not one word about Nandi customs," he said. "The Holy Spirit will do the correcting of the custom." (Baxter 1982:P.I.). Bryson advised her never to speak against female circumcision. And she does not recall missionaries speaking on the subject during those early days. Nor does she remember missionaries speaking against male circumcision.

These examples could be multiplied in greater number than this small book could contain. The fact is that in many places and under many circumstances the African believers did participate in the decisions made by the early Christian church regarding African culture. A report on the Christian approach to the **kithitu** in Ukambani is a vivid demonstration that the church elders in fact did play a key role in deciding what should be done about some of the African traditions. Harmon Nixon, an A.I.M. missionary among the Akamba, gave this report to Ralph Davis, the A.I.M. leader in the States. The full presentation of the letter gives a balanced perspective on the subject.

The **kithitu** is a charm made from the horn of an antelope over which the Akamba take oaths in law courts. Up until very recently the local Government at Machakos would not allow Christians to take oaths on the Bible in civil law suits. To discerning Christians of which there is an ever growing number, 'an idol is nothing in the world.' They laugh at people fearing a horn filled with trash. In civil law suits the crafty heathen have often defeated the unfortunate Christians who by, ecclesiastical ruling were formerly prevented from swearing on the **kithitu.** Failure to swear on the **kithitu** is to the heathen tribunal elders 'prima facie' evidence of guilt. The Ukambani Regional Council ruled that Christians in Machakos District who had been sued at law by pagans could take an oath on the **kithitu.**

In Kitui District the **kithitu** has much more sinister meaning than it does here (Machakos). Those taking the oath in Kitui must remove their clothes, while taking the oath. Most Christians in Kitui still have a certain amount of faith in evil spirits and witchcraft. For a Christian in Kitui, to take an oath on a **kithitu** would be to defile his conscience. Further more, in Kitui, Christians can take oaths on the Bible which was not permitted in this district till after the above ruling was passed. I may say that the rule of the Regional Council applied to Machakos District only. Our oldest and most spiritual men unanimously supported it.

Scripturally, I think it is better 'to swear not at all,' but for a Mukamba to lose a law suit just because of not being allowed to take an oath is unthinkable. Now that our Machakos people can swear on the Bible the **kithitu** need not 'be eaten'. (Nixon 1940)

This letter demonstrates that the African Christian elders participated in the decision making process. It demonstrates that the decisions regarding **kithitu** differed in Kitui and Machakos, showing that uniformity was not required by the missionaries. The different decisions arose in part from different circumstances and different perspectives of the Christians. Harmon Nixon reflects a sympathetic understanding of the African Christian's plight and an openness to various possible approaches.

## Colonial Context

On the one hand, historical investigation demonstrates that African Christians from the beginning of the Church in Africa participated in many of the decisions regarding the biblical approach to their African culture. Furthermore, many missionaries did in fact value various aspects of African culture. Thus we affirm that the perspective of such African scholars as Muga (Muga 1975:100) and missionary scholars as Cope (Cope 1979:27) is not balanced. We cannot simply state that older missionaries considered African culture, religion and customs to be all of the devil. That is not factual.

On the other hand, this book would not be balanced either if we concluded our discussion at this point. We must note that generalizations about missionaries and their approach to Africans and African culture are as dangerous as generalizations are in general. We must remember that missionaries differed greatly among themselves.

Take the question of clothes. We have seen that some missionaries tried to prevent Africans from adopting European clothes. Still other missionaries participated in the call for Africans to change their apparel. The A.I.M. missionaries among the Nandi are a case in point. The traditional dress was goat skins and beads. The missionaries encouraged the Nandi to remove the beads since they were dirty and filled with lice. Since the beads went up to the elbows and neck, it was not possible to wash the body with them on. Likewise, the goat skins were smelly, having been rubbed with fat. When Nandi women came to church with their traditional dress, the other African Christian ladies would move over from them because of the smell of the skins. The removal of such traditional garb was not mandatory but encouraged by the earlier missionaries. Later missionaries were more reticent in advising the Nandi to remove the skins and beads. But change did come(Baxter 1982:P.I).

Morever, we cannot escape the whole colonial context in which the Gospel was first preached and the church planted here in Africa. Missionaries who came from the West had enjoyed many of the conveniences and advances in human knowledge which were not known in Africa. They had not been trained in cross cultural understanding of other peoples. Their reaction to African culture was therefore, in many ways, negative. That was part of the whole world view of the westerner during the colonial era.

Apart from the culturally sensitized person today, our reaction is not different from theirs. African missionaries serving among "primitive" peoples today who are naked and living with far fewer conveniences than back home, speak freely of their backwardness. Regrettably, there was an air of superiority among many missionaries who readily assumed the superiority of their own western culture and the inferiority of the African culture. Without the benefits of cross cultural studies preparing them for missionary service, they frequently failed to understand and appreciate the "strange" features of the culture.

It is doubtful whether we should presume today that we would have responded differently than did those early missionaries. The whole context from which they came and into which they were plunged lended itself toward an air of superiority. Elspeth Huxley describes the Kenya scene at the turn of the century.

> By European standards Kenya in 1900 was 'wholly primitive.' Its scattered peoples, grouped into separate and mutually hostile tribes, were pagan, frequently nomadic, ignorant of the outside world and of such simple devices as plough, the wheel, the pump, the loom, the coin; they had evolved no alphabet, built no cities, made no roads; their tool was the digging stick, their dress the skin, their weapon the spear (Huxley 1970:I,v).

Cagnolo, a Roman Catholic missionary to the Gikuyu, expressed "pity for those poor slaves of ignorance." He then declared, "It is an obligation upon us civilized peoples to put these phantasms to flight..." (Cagnolo 1930:189) While Europeans have grown in their own understanding of the dark spots in their own western culture and gained new appreciation for the values of African traditional culture, the earlier missionaries did not enjoy these advantages. They were children of their age, even as we are today. As Huxley reminds us, almost every European held to the same belief.

"Civilization was good, barbarism was bad; Europeans were civilized, Africans were not; ergo, the European incursion that carried with it Christianity, literacy and the PAX BRITANNICA and an end to famines and epidemics could be nothing but a boon to Africans. It was as simple as that." (Huxley 1970:I,v) Only in this context can we understand the attitude and behaviour of those early missionaries. One can find all too many examples of crude superiority expressed in a variety of ways.

13

And so we can say that although the African believers often did play a significant role in various decisions regarding African traditional customs, all too often the missionaries were first among equals in the decision making process. Moreover, all too often critical questions with regard to African customs were imposed on the Africans instead of allowing the Holy Spirit over the course of time to develop a consensus among the believers.

We have previously seen that the Protestant Missions in Kenya were evangelical and sought to cooperate together on many policy decisions pertaining to African culture. We can find among those missions unfortunate examples of missionaries imposing their theological understanding on the African believers.

## Example of Female Circumcision

One tragic example is that of female circumcision. All the Alliance Missions (C.M.S., C.S.M., A.I.M. and Methodist), without dissent, ruled that anyone who underwent female circumcision or any Christian parent who consented to or assisted in the circumcision of the daughter would be disciplined. They all required that Christians before baptism take a vow against female circumcision (K.M.C. 1930). Female circumcision was frequently referred to as "sexual mutilation of girls." The missionary medical doctors were foremost in their opposition to this traditional practice. This consensus of missionary thinking against clitoridectomy was based on medical grounds, not moral. Because of the physical mutilation, the suffering and mental anguish imposed on the girls, female circumcision was opposed.

The Alliance was not alone. The Kenya Missionary Council composed of all Protestant Missions working in Kenya went on record that their conviction was that "it is the duty of the Christian Church to impress upon all its members and adherents that the sexual mutilation of girls or women is contrary to the teachings of Christ." (K.M.C. 1930)

The typed pamphlet in English and Kikuyu prepared for the Alliance of Missionary Societies by Dr. Philip of the Church of Scotland Mission on the subject of female circumcision was also submitted to the Kenya Missionary Council. In 1927 the K.M.C. agreed to print the pamphlet, "preferably by the Africa Inland Mission, Kijabe, for distribution throughout Kikuyu Reserve." (K.M.C. 1927).

Prohibition against female circumcision was enforced first of all through church membership requirements. Before baptism the Church of Scotland Mission asked the candidates nine questions, including this one.

> Do you resolve anew to reject Satan and all his work, with all evil lusts; and that you will eschew all things not agreeable to the Word of God, such as things pertaining to departed spirits, witchcraft, divination, sexual immorality, intoxicating liquor, evil songs and female circumcision? (C.S. 1926)

Once a person became a member of the church, he or she could be disciplined by either submitting to female circumcision as a girl or by permitting female cir-

14

cumcision as responsible adults. This was true both in the Africa Inland Mission and the Church of Scotland Mission (Barlow 1925).

Further pressure was brought to bear on the peoples by prohibiting female circumcision among girls registered in mission schools. This became a critical problem among the Gikuyu who first saw much of their good land taken by the colonialists. Later their traditional customs were threatened by preventing girls from attending mission schools if they underwent female cirumcision.

To enforce this stand the A.I.M. drew up a document which all evangelists, teachers and other church and school leaders were required to sign among the Gikuyu. The A.I.M. was prepared to sacrifice a large portion of her membership in order "to purify and strengthen the church." Eventually, all the A.I.M. Gikuyu Christians were compelled to sign the loyalty pledge or be expelled from the church (Sandgren 1976:182).

The result of this united mission policy together with all the other grave problems related to land, was the development of a crisis within Kenya during the 1920's. The A.I.M called for a special conference at Kijabe in October 1920 with no pre-arranged agenda and no closing date. The missionaries were to give themselves to prayer for revival until satisfied that God had heard their prayers. Included in the trouble that concerned the missionaries was "the Thuku Movement which for a time threatened to sweep the whole missionary movement in Kenya off its feet..." (Stauffacher 1927) Letters by the missionaries reflect the tension of those days. "These are critical days in Kenya," wrote Hulda Stumpf. "Lawlessness, insubordination, rebellion, disobedience and every other modifying term of sin in the catalogue among the people." (Stumpf 1927)

While the various Protestant missions took a uniform and steadily tougher line against female circumcision, various individual missionaries were uncertain about the approach they should take. John Stauffacher, an A.I.M. missionary among the Masai, wrote this:

> My opinion about female circumcision...The whole of Kenya is stirred up, as it has now gone from the Church to the Government, an attempt having been made largely by the missionaries to make a civil law prohibiting it throughout the Colony. There is no question in my mind as to whether or not it should be stopped. It is a brutal custom...but the question that is puzzling some of us is how to stop it. Some of the churches are expelling members wholesale, so that where there was a large congregation only four or five members remain. The Scottish Mission are I believe even demanding a thumb print signifying their opposition to female circumcision, or expulsion from the church. Kijabe I understand is taking the same stand, and I am told that we will soon be required to do the same, in which case as matters stand we will have no church at all. I agree that no one should be received into the Church who is in favor of it, and also that no one should be allowed to remain who had any part in it, but that men and women who have been in the Church for so many years, some as much as twenty, and all that time in good standing, and now suddenly should be told they must

15

change their minds or get out, I can't quite make up my mind as to whether that is right or not. I feel that it is a bit too pre-mature, for to use a very poor argument these very men and women know that in some European congregations there are members who commit adultery, and no finger print is required of them. Of course what is wrong is wrong, but the fact that it has been allowed through a long period of years, seems to me requires care, lest we drive the mature Christians wholly away from us, at any rate let us begin first with the Europeans, for as some natives told me a few days ago, that if the white men will promise not to take their women for immoral purposes they will promise to stop circumcision, in fact many are using the argument that that is the very reason why the white men are demanding it, not very much of a compliment to the white race... (Stauffacher 1929)

Hulda Stumpf from Kijabe referred to a Joshua Mucai who along with others "was prohibited from teaching and was excommunicated FOREVER [emphasis original], the sentence read, unless he was willing to confess his wrong and swear allegiance to the white man and his rulings. The confession was sorrow for allowing his daughter to be circumcized." (Stumpf 1927) She observed that the teaching why some customs are to be avoided and others utilized while others should be purified has "to be done in LOVE [emphasis original], and not be legislation."

Indeed, this seems to have become the problem. The church in her sphere and the government in theirs used legislation to enforce the prohibition of female circumcision. Dr. Arthur of the Church of Scotland Mission resigned from the Executive Committee of the Legislative Council because they could not agree with him. John Stauffacher expressed concern that the Africans may believe "we missionaries are the law makers of the country" and that we are "responsible for laws which compel them against their will." (Stauffacher 1929)

For the A.I.M., the female circumcision controversy reached a crisis when Hulda Stumpf, 64 years old, was suffocated and forcibly circumcized in her own house at Kijabe on January 2, 1930. The irony of this tragedy is that Hulda Stumpf is the one who on several occasions raised doubts whether the mission policy concerning female circumcision was correct.

It is true of course that some African Christians also opposed clitoridectomy, though not without dissent. At the Conference of Kikuyu Church Elders in 1929 they agreed with one dissenting voice, that female circumcision is evil and should be abandoned by all Christians. They also agreed by a large majority that everyone submitting to the rite or requiring to submit to it, would be suspended from churches everywhere. Nine Kikuyu elders disagreed with this last resolution, advising the churches to go more slowly in this problem (C.K.E. 1929).

But this advice by the minority of Kikuyu church elders to move more slowly on the question was not followed. Instead the decisions made to prohibit female circumcision were enforced. The A.I.M. Conference made the

16

ruling that "all Church members and Catechumens who would not publicly declare themselves opposed to female circumcision, cut of [sic] their relation to Church and Class." When Stauffacher returned to Narok with this mission decision which needed implementation, he returned "with fear and trembling." He informed the Masai Christians of this decision.

Imagine the horror that came over me when only two boys stood by us, and the rest in a mass withdrew, threating [sic] to take possession of the church, and organize to suit themselves, calling us false teachers, and that they alone stood for the truth. You at home who cannot see the defiant look on their faces, cannot possibly realize what this means to us, when men whose sincerity has never been doubted, and who have prayed and worked with us some of them more than twenty years, suddenly without warning turn and become our deadliest enemies (Stauffacher 1930a).

John Stauffacher lamented,

...and I cannot help but feel sometimes that somewhere we have made a tremendous mistake, when it becomes necessary for us to force Christians (and I believe most of them are Christians) who have only so recently come out of the rankest heathenism. I don't see now how we can do differently, but I doubt if we should have done much harm if we had agreed that since female circumcision must go, we would be patient and work and pray against it, rather than that we should make a rule that severs them from church membership. I am afraid hundreds of them will never return (Stauffacher 1930b).

While he states that the decision against female circumcision was "unanimous among all missionaries of all Societies," he declares, "I can't help but admit that my heart goes out strongly sometimes to the natives, although I know from our viewpoint they are wholly wrong." This "huge mistake" has played "terrific havoc" in the Church so that "as far as the human eye can see now our work here is a complete wreck." (Stauffacher 1930c)

The result was a massive exodus from all the Gikuyu churches and schools with only a handful of loyalists remaining. Githumu and Kijabe "were reduced to two or three loyal families each." (Sandgren 1976:237) Only a handful of children attended school. Only a few dozen Gikuyu families remained·faithful to the A.I.M. in the early months of 1930, compared to 500 Gikuyu members in 1926. When 95% of the Gikuyu A.I.M. Christians had boycotted the church for the year 1930, attempts were made to rescind earlier decisions by allowing students to return to school without signing a pledge against female circumcision. But very few returned.

A cleavage had occurred within the mission founded churches, between the **kirore** (the older converts prior to World War I who had extended contact with the missionaries on the mission stations) and the **athome** (the Christians on the

17

out-stations who became more closely indentified with the Gikuyu in their concerns over European intrusion into Gikuyu land and customs). And this cleavage remained with permanent results.

The colonial policy regarding the land thus became the initial problem which led to agitation against colonial rule. But the mission policy regarding schools, used to enforce repudiation of female circumcision, became the torch that lit the fires which eventually led to the ouster of British rule and a massive exodus of Christians from mission founded schools.

Since missions were the exclusive administrators of schools among the Gikuyu, the people had no where to turn but to establish their own schools. And founding of independent schools went hand in hand with the founding of independent churches, all closely linked with the Kikuyu Central Associaton which advocated "no intervention of the white missionaries." (Leakey 1952:91) The Gikuyu Independent Churches were a by-product of the independent schools, since schools and churches were inseparable (Murray Brown 1972:141).

From our perspective today this mission policy regarding female circumcision was a tragic mistake. Instead of "purifying" the church, the churches were emptied. Instead of strengthening the Christians, they were weakened. For instead of attending churches where the Word of God was fully taught, they became adherents of the African independent churches. In the place of the mission churches and schools, the African Independent Pentecostal Church in Africa was formed in 1925 with their independent schools, and the African Orthodox Church was established in 1928 with their independent schools.

From the viewpoint of evangelicals who know these independent churches from within, there is a grave lack of spiritual vitality and a lack of faithfulness to the Word of God among the churches. Politics plays an important role in the life of the church and we frequently read of clashes between parties within the churches, necessitating government intervention and supervision of the elections. Yet a very large portion of Gikuyu who once belonged to the mission founded churches, together with their descendants, are now identified with these African Independent Churches. And ironically, while female circumcision is strongly advocated by the older members, the practice is rapidly declining.

As evangelicals we firmly believe that the Spirit of the Living God indwells every believer. Jesus Christ is the Lord of His Body which is the Church. While conversion brings about radical change through the lordship of Jesus Christ, growth in grace is a slow process which involves a life time of maturing.

Female circumcision is unlike murder or adultery, sins specifically and clearly forbidden by the Word of God. Seldom did the mission ever try to base their objection to female circumcision on religious reasons. Rather, it was the physical aspect which brought on the opposition, the pain and suffering of the girls, the mutilation of the body, together with the psychological effects. The decision to oppose female circumcision was made primarily by the missionaries without due consideration of the conscience of the believers and their understanding of the will of God for their lives.

18

It may appear to some that the issue of female circumcision belongs to antiquity. The practice is disappearing. The government of Kenya occasionally speaks out against the custom. During some extensive research of mine several years ago I was led to believe by various individuals that female circumcision is indeed an irrelevant issue today. But such is not the case. Female circumcision may not be publicly acknowledged by many. Perhaps the practice is not known by many or not readily acknowledged. But recently we have come across reports of hospitals and private medical offices in which girls seek the operation of clitoridectomy. And we have heard of girls who feel so deeply the need for clitoridectomy, perhaps induced by their boy friends, that they seek to operate on themselves with horrible physical and emotional effects. The Christian Church in Africa today needs to address itself to this issue. What does God have to say to Christian believers who still feel a need for this traditional rite? The missionaries gave their verdict years ago. What word of God do evangelical African believers have for those in our midst who feel a continued need for this traditional rite?

Herein is a most important reason for African Christian Theology today. Each generation of Christians must consider anew God's will for their lives in their own living context. For the African Church today, there is an ever greater need since so many of the practices and beliefs of the churches today were not made primarily by African believers but by expatriates.

## Example of Polygamy

Another example of this need for African Christian Theology is polygamy. As the missionaries presented the claims of Christ to the Africans, the inevitable question arose over polygamy. It is of interest that the first recorded statement on polygamy by the Africa Inland Mission in 1903 is virtually identical to the decision of all the independent churches which have broken off of the A.I.M. founded Church, the Africa Inland Church. In 1903, soon after Charles Hurlburt, the new Director of the A.I.M., arrived in Kenya, he made the following observations when there was an initial influx of Gikuyu converts at Kijabe. Hurlburt wrote,

> Many problems are arising needing peculiar guidance. One is the question of polygamy. Kikuvi, for instance, has several wives, all bought before he knew the things of God. He was willing to put them all away, but by our advice kept them, because to drive them away would be cruel injustice, and would force them to lives of shame and slavery. His retaining them has led all but one to a definite, public acceptance of Jesus as Saviour. If driven away they must have hated the Gospel and its teachings. A large majority of the mission feels that the only right basis is to insist that converts take no more wives, if young, that they marry but one, but the wives shall not be put away unless they are willing to go and marry another man. We may change this basis in after years, but this is our present light. While we shall set a premium on monogamy by withholding official privileges from those who have more than one wife. (H & D, VII, 4, 1903:19)

19

We are here informed that the Director of the A.I.M. and the majority of missionaries in 1903 believed that monogamy was the Christian norm. But that no polygamist who became a believer should be required to put away any of his wives. In fact, the Director of the A.I.M. refused the offer by Kikuvi who was willing to put away his wives if that was required.

Within ten years this all changed. The Continuation Committee of the Kikuyu Conference in 1913 recommended that no person living in polygamy shall have the Lord's Supper administered to him (C.C.K.C. 1918). This indeed became the standard of all those Mission Churches which dreamed of merging to form one united Christian Church in British East Africa.

The reasons for this change are not known, though we can speculate. Whereas Martin Luther and Melanthon held that monogamy was not obligatory under every circumstance, that whatever was permitted by the law of Moses, remained lawful today, John Calvin disagreed. Calvin forbade polygamy, saying that the patriarchs were guilty of sin (Barrett 1968:19).

Now as a matter of historical fact, there was a close comradeship between the A.I.M. missionaries and those of the Church of Scotland Mission. Their mission headquarters were relatively close together. At times the A.I.M. conference invited C.S.M. missionaries to speak to the missionaries. Dr. Arthur of C.S.M., a powerful person, became a prominent voice within the Alliance of Missionary Societies. It may very well be that the strong convictions of John Arthur, heir of Calvinism in the Church of Scotland, and prominent in the Alliance of Missions, made a strong impact on the missionaries, regarding polygamy.

Whatever the reason for the united stand by Kenyan missions against polygamy, a very significant development has occurred. The African Independent Churches which have broken from the Africa Inland Church all agree in their dissent with the A.I.M. on their approach to polygamy.

Now the contemporary view of African Independent Churches by many scholars is that they represent truly indigenous Christianity. It is said that the Christianity brought to Africa was a westernized form which the Independent Churches are now Africanizing. For instance, Muga affirms that "in the past few decades the Africans have rejected the over-westernized form of Christianity and this rejection has manifested itself in the formation of African Independent church movements which have all along reinforced national political movements." (Muga 1975:Preface)

A study of those African Independent Churches which have broken from the Africa Inland Church reflect only some modest adjustments with regard to belief and practice. There are no independent churches which broke from the Kalenjin A.I.C., none from the Luo A.I.C., though David Barrett erroneously reported that in 1954 The Voice of Salvation and Healing Church broke off from the Africa Inland Mission (Barrett 1973:188, 189). Almost all of the churches which broke from the Africa Inland Church are among the Akamba, except for the African Christian Church and Schools which broke from the Gikuyu A.I.C. in 1947 over the issue of inadequate emphasis on schools by the A.I.M. These Akamba African Independent Churches are four in number: the African Brotherhood Church, Good News Church of Africa, Ebenezer Gospel Church and the African Church.

All these independent churches follow basically the same doctrinal beliefs as the Africa Inland Church. One who worships in any of these independent African churches sees little difference from the pattern of divine worship practised in the Africa Inland Church. Furthermore, they adhere to the same approach to African customs and culture as the mother church and mission. There is one exception-their approach to the problem of polygamy.

None of these African Independent Churches embrace polygamy as the Christian ideal. Nor do they allow any polygamist to hold church office. But they all agree without exception that a polygamist who is converted can be baptized and admitted to the Lord's Table without being compelled to give up all his wives except his first. The striking thing is that they all agree so completely on this issue, and that this approach is what was first advocated by the Africa Inland Mission in 1903.

Today the problem of polygamy continually surfaces in the various councils of the Africa Inland Church and among other mission churches. Here is a problem that has been inherited by today's believers from the founding fathers of the mission and church. What would God have His people do today concerning polygamy?

Traditionalism is a very real evil. To continue following a belief or practice simply because our forefathers did it in the church is not biblical. Each generation of believers needs to examine its own faith in the light of what God has taught in the Word of God. Because of non-biblical traditions, entrenched in the Roman Catholic Church, the Reformers found it necessary to contend for the faith and suffer the consequences of excommunication. What is necessary today is for Christian believers to turn to the Scriptures, time and time again, to have their understanding of these problems reformed by the Word of God.

Hindsight is always better than foresight. We are ever guilty of a kind of "generational-centrism," in which we judge past generations by our own standards and insights. Even as ethnocentric people judge other cultures by their own standards, thinking their own ways are the best, so every generation tends to weigh and assess former generations by their own values and standard of enlightment. There are many today who wish the missions and their churches in Africa had not followed their course of action against female circumcision. And many wish that our approach to polygamy had been a bit different, perhaps that which is represented by the African Independent Churches mentioned above. But the past is past and cannot be undone.

We are reminded of a Kikamba proverb which says, "You can rear a ram, then it butts you." Where would we be today if the earlier missionary pioneers had not come to Africa? We are the rams which they have reared. It is all too easy for us, their children, offspring who owe our lives to them, to turn around and be ungrateful to them, butting them until it hurts. We pluck out the speck from their

21

eyes, forgetting that we ourselves are not without the beams in our own eyes. Jesus said, "Blessed are the merciful, for they shall obtain mercy." We all stand in need of mercy. We would do well to display mercy to our forefathers, grateful for the rich heritage we have received from them.

Nevertheless, the Christian Church that has been planted in Africa is not bound by the teachings and convictions of her forbears. We are bound instead to Jesus Christ and His Word found in the Bible. We are responsible to shape our lives according to the will of God as we understand it in the Bible. God has no grandchildren. Each generation must be born again by the Spirit. And God's children cannot eat the manna from a generation ago. We ourselves must feed daily on the Scriptures and seek to understand God's will for our lives.

For these reasons African Christian Theology is a necessity today for a vital, healthy, growing, effective church.

# CONCLUSION

We now may summarize the many and varied reasons why African Christian Theology is a necessity today.

1. The Holy Spirit who indwells the whole Body of Christ worldwide has promised to guide His people into a knowledge of God's truth.

The process of reflecting upon God's revelation in the light of one's context and then communicating that theological understanding to others has been a continuing process for the past 2,000 years. This process must also continue in Africa because the Holy Spirit will lead all of us into all truth. Jesus Christ is Lord of all and His Spirit indwells all of His people.

2. No Christian wherever he is found and no body of believers whatever their location can live on traditions, even holy, Christian traditions, without a personal encounter with God and His Word.

While all Christians are inter-dependent and while all particular churches are inter-related to one another throughout time and space, each body of believers must seek for themselves God's will for their lives. To depend upon theological conclusions of another generation without seeking out the truth for oneself is to eat stale bread without proper nourishment.

3. The Church of Jesus Christ in Africa must seek God's answer to her problems and needs unique to her own context.

Each individual Christian and each fellowship of believers finds itself in a unique stage of maturity. While we can learn and benefit from others in hearing what other Christians are doing about certain situations which confront them, we ought not mimic them and parrot their solutions. Our solutions to our problems as we understand them from God's Word may in fact be similar to the solutions found elsewhere, but we should find those solutions through our own reflection on our context and in the light of God's Word.

While the Word of God is true for all people everywhere so that we all must conform to that one system of truth in the Word of God, each context has its own

22

peculiar problems and potential. The African Christian Church has unique problems which are not faced by any other church in the same manner. Therefore, the African Christian Church must seek from God in the Scriptures through the illumination of the Holy Spirit the resolution to those problems.

4.    The Body of Christ in Africa, through a reflection upon the Bible in their context, may be able to contribute to a fuller understanding of God's revelation for all people and thereby contribute toward a fuller, more balanced Christian theology for the Church universal.

Because of our own limitations in understanding the whole counsel of the Word of God, we tend to focus on certain truths which are made particularly relevant due to our own situation. Thus our own unique understanding of Scriptures may contribute to the understanding of Scriptures by the Church universal. In other words, our cultural and historical context may enable us to comprehend some truth of the Word of God which is not fully appreciated by other people of God in different contexts. Therefore, we have an obligation to contribute our understanding of God's revelation to the whole of theological reflection by the universal Church.

5.    Church renewal, necessary for every generation of Christians, is dependent upon a prayerful study of God's Word within each given context of need.

Only through the study of the Word of God can each generation of believers be revived. Revival and renewal of each believer in each generation necessitates a reflection of their own lives in the light of God's Word. The end result will be a genuinely inspired African Christian Theology which brings renewal and blessing by the working of the Holy Spirit.

As we study the history of the Christian Church we discover that unless each generation of believers comes to know God in a new and personal way, that branch of the church becomes stale in her love for God, stagnant in her spiritual growth and eventually sterile in her Christian life. Church renewal is absolutely essential in each generation. And that cannot take place apart from earnest prayer and a study of God's Word in each given context.

6.    For the Church in Africa to be well established as a genuinely indigenous Christian Church, it is imperative for the believers to think through their Christian Faith for themselves by the power of the Holy Spirit and in the light of the Holy Scriptures.

Given the history of the Christian Church in Africa, there are many cultural issues which have either not been studied in the light of God's Word or have not been thought through by the sons and daughters of Africa. Many of our problems faced in Africa were either not addressed in the past, or were inadequately considered by the founding fathers. This calls for urgent consideration by the present generation.

7.    Christianity in Africa must be properly contextualized so that believers will feel at home with their Christian faith and non-believers will be attracted by its beauty.

Whether murals portraying the life of Jesus Christ should reflect an African background or not, it is essential that there be much continuity between traditional African culture and their newly found Christian faith. All that is good in traditional Africa and all that can be purified and utilized for the glory of God should be assimilated into the expression and communication of the Gospel of Jesus Christ.

Of course, everything must be measured by the standard of Holy Writ. But there is much truth and goodness in traditional African culture derived by the grace of God which can and must be incorporated into Christianity in Africa. The whole purpose is two-fold: to help believers find delight and joy in expressing their faith in Christ:-true fulfillment and a sense of belonging; and secondly, to commuicate the Gospel to the unbelievers in such a manner that they are drawn to Jesus Christ, the Saviour of the world, yes, and particularly of Africa.

8. The Body of Christ in Africa is directly responsible to Jesus Christ, the Head of the Church, and not to some foreign bishop or ecclesiastical body.

On the one hand, we as members of the Body of Christ, must be rightly related to the Universal Christian Church. We believe in the apostolicity of the Church, not based on external descent by ordination but on the internal assent to the teaching of the apostles of Jesus Christ as found in the New Testament. Any church that falls away from assent to that which has been taught by the Apostles ceases to be part of the Holy Catholic Church.

On the other hand, the disciples of Jesus Christ are primarily and ultimately responsible to Christ Himself. We reject all forms of eccelesiastical imperialism whereby foreigners in one continent control the faith and practice of believers in another continent. Jesus Christ has granted to each believer and to the believers collectively in each particular church the priesthood whereby we have immediate access to the Father by the Spirit apart from any other human intermediary. We have divine illumination by the Holy Spirit as we seek to know God's will through His Word.

Having affirmed the necessity of African Christian Theology we would note that it would seem better to speak of Christian theology (or theologies) in Africa rather than African Christian Theology. What we want is a biblical theology properly related to each given context. So we would prefer to speak of Evangelical Christian Theology in the context of Africa. Generally, we do not speak of European Christian Theology or American Christian Theology. There are many diverse Christian theologies in the west. Furthermore, Europe is as diverse as Africa with scores of "tribes" with traditional hostilities between them. And these diverse theologies in Europe seem to be unrelated to the cultural differences among the European "tribes."

Moreover, we may find in the future greater tendencies to divide our theologies on the basis of various peculiar emphases not necessarily related to cultural origins. Hence we find Liberation Theology, Barthian Theology, Pentecostal Theology, Arminian Theology, Black Theology, Reformed Theology, Lutheran Theology etc. We read that African Christian Theology is divided into three brands: African Inculturation Theology, South African Black Theology and African Liberation Theology (Ukpong 1984). We might note that Liberation Theology was adopted from Latin America and Black Theology from the United States. Apparently, though each of these theologies originated in specific historical and foreign contexts, their theological bases are not dependent upon any relationship to those contexts, since all these diverse theologies are believed and followed in scores of nations and in a wide range of contexts.

We would call for an evangelical theology for the African context which reflects the great evangelical truths which have united evangelicals through the centuries and apply these to the African context. We need to continue relating the great evangelical truths of biblical revelation to the ever changing contexts found in Africa. Only as we take the written Word of God as our absolute and final authority will we conclude with an evangelical theology for Africa and rightly related to the historic creeds of Christianity. However, what may happen more quickly is that various theological emphases represented in our evangelical churches will become incarnated in the African culture. Thus our evangelical theologies incarnated in the African culture, will be related to those great historic theological emphases in the universal church.

For these reasons, we prefer speaking of Christian theology or theologies in Africa. Regardless of the term we may use, we have surely demonstrated that there are many reasons why the Christians in Africa need to address various issues which are specifically African in nature. African Christians also need to communicate their theological reflections in a uniquely African manner for effective communication. Thus the Christian theology developed in Africa will have a distinctive African stamp while ever holding to the one apostolic faith. And in this sense we speak of African Christian Theology.

# Chapter 2

# THE HISTORY

## THE ORIGINS OF AFRICAN
## CHRISTIAN THEOLOGY

### Originated with the First Proclamation of the Gospel

In one sense African Christian Theology is as old as Christianity itself in Africa. From the very beginning when the Gospel was first preached by missionaries and the peoples believed and received the Gospel, there was African Christian Theology. The Gospel took root in the hearts of the Africans as the Word of God was effectively communicated, meeting the needs of men and women. The African believers began to share their faith with others, using their own language and culture as the medium of communication. They began to formulate their Christian faith in African terms.

In any successful effort to communicate the Gospel to a people across cultural boundaries there must be some measure of relating biblical truths to the known practices and beliefs of the people. Without translation, no communication is possible. And theology is translation (cf. Sundkler 1960:281).

Baeta observes, "my view is that if the gospel is being presented relevantly and with a full effectiveness, i.e., in such a manner that under African conditions and circumstances it is doing its gospel work- then its complete indigenization has taken place..." (Baeta 1964:21).

Everyone recognizes the phenomenal growth of the Christian Church in Africa. In a very real sense the Gospel has been understood, received and believed. The Gospel has met deeply felt needs. Therefore, we conclude that a significant degree of indigenization of Christianity has taken place in Africa because the Gospel is doing its saving work of grace.

"Theology" is a discourse about God, a study of God, sometimes referred to as a science. Any "God-talk," any effort to speak about our understanding of God, is theology (Fashole-Luke 1974a:100). In the Christian context theology is inseparable from the Scripture. The Christian Church has historically believed that the Bible is the Word of God. Thus theology is man's understanding of God's revelation of Himself in the Scripture. Theology may simply be defined as the application of the Word of God to all areas of life. Theology is done whenever people reflect on divine revelation and communicate their understanding of God's revelation to others.

As Adeyemo has said, Doing Theology for evangelicals "is an obedient spirit-led reflection upon God's revelatory words and acts, culminating in Jesus Christ, an honest application of the same to our lives, and consequent sincere communication of it for perfecting the saints for the work of the ministry (see Ezra 7:10; Eph. 4:12)." (1983:147)

All too often theology is equated with professional scholars writing books on theology for one another. A measure of a theologian is his ability to interact with philosophers and theologians who write in many different languages. This view is reflected by Agbeti, who comments, "A 'theology' is not technically 'theology' when the experience about God had not been systematically, critically and scholarly interpreted or articulated." (1972:7) If we restrict theology to the elite writing discourses on theology, then indeed, African Christian Theology is of recent origins.

But theology is more basic than that. Theology not only can be done but in actual practice is done by all believers, whatever their educational level may be, when they reflect and think about their Christian faith and communicate that to others. As Tienou has observed, theology "is reflection on God's self-disclosure contained in the Scripture with the purpose of generating the knowledge of God and better obedience." (1983:98)

As such, Africans have been reflecting on the Scriptures since the Bible was first translated into the vernacular languages. All Bible translations are interpretations of the text from which the Bible is being translated. Anyone familiar with the dynamics of translation recognizes that there is no exact equivalence in any two languages. The translator must use his God given judgment as to what words to use and how to express those original thoughts. In every instance the Bible translations into the variouus African vernaculars were made with the assistance of African Christians.

A case in point is the translation of the Nandi Bible, the first complete Bible translated into a Kenyan vernacular language. In 1929 the Africa Inland Mission Field Council in Kenya appointed two men to translate the Nandi Bible: Stuart Bryson, the A.I.M. missionary, and Samuel Gimnyige, the Nandi pastor. They were co-workers in this task. For ten years these and other Nandi believers worked on the translation. They began with no Nandi grammar or dictionary even of the simplest kind. In 1933, the Brysons who then were the only A.I.M missionaries in Nandi land, were "still collecting Nandi words on scraps of paper which were kept in bundles in a biscuit-tin." (Bryson 1959:74)

But the Nandi Christians themselves played the pivotal role in the translation. Pastor Gimnyige worked steadily with Bryson all week long, before bicycling back to Ndulele on the week-end to conduct the work at the school and lead in the Sunday services. Others shared in the work including Reuben Arap Seroney and Reuben Arap Lagat. Sometimes they would struggle over the best way to translate the Bible. Throughout the days and weeks they would search for the best ways to communicate what God has said in the Bible. Sometimes the solution would be found suddenly while listening to the Nandi speak in the village or by observing some traditional practice.

The New Testament was published in Australia. Later in May 1939 the British and Foregn Bible Society printed the whole Nandi Bible, the first vernacular Bible in Kenya. While Bible translation may not appear at first glance to be doing theology, it is in fact nothing less. For the whole process of translating God's Word into the Nandi language necessitated reflection on what God meant in His Word and how best to communicate that to the Nandi in their culture.

"Oral Theology" is the interpretation of the biblical message through sermons, teachings, prayers, discussions, songs, witnessing and any oral communication. Mbiti is correct when he says, "glimpses of African Theology may be found in the total African response, in word and action, to the gospel." (Dickson 1974:205)

Many times the impression is given in missionary histories that the expatriate missionaries were the chief ones who evangelized and spread the Good News of Jesus Christ. But this is contrary to the facts. The African believers themselves were the chief agents in the rapid spread of the Gospel.

The most important agent in evangelism in the Africa Inland Mission was the African Christian who served as evangelist and school teacher. From the earliest days of the A.I.M. there was the recognition that "evangelization must be done by the Africans themselves," as Peter Cameron Scott wrote in his diary (Miller n.d.:43). The vision was to train the Africans to be pastors so that they could staff the stations in a few years and the missionaries be freed to move on to unreached territory (H & D, VII, 5, 1903:12, 13).

John Stauffacher, the Extension Director of the A.I.M., gave an address to the A.I.M. Missionary Conference in 1912 in which he affirmed, "All we can hope for is to train those who shall do the work while we spread from tribe to tribe...Unless we hold continually before the native that the work is theirs, and we have come simply to show them how to do it, we shall never make much progress." (H & D, Oct. - Dec., 1912). Thus the number of evangelists, employed by the A.I.M., continued to grow. In 1922 there were 200 African evangelists, and by the late 1930's a reported 1,600 "native evangelists" working among 25 tribes in East and Central Africa.

Bible Schools played an important part in the preparation of pastors and evangelists. Within the Kenyan Africa Inland Church today the strongest element by far is among the Akamba. The reason for this cannot be wholly attributed to the number of missionaries labouring in Ukambani, though that is one element. The fact is that 25 years after the A.I.M. began working in Kenya, the Gikuyu A.I.C. was the largest, the Luo A.I.C. the second largest, and the Akamba the third largest. Many factors played their part.

But the significant difference seems to be the Ukamba Bible Institute begun in 1928. The Akamba Church is the only part of the A.I.C. which has had its own vernacular Bible Institute for any sustained length of time. Moffat Bible School at

Kijabe, begun in 1929, was taught in Kiswahili and intended for the Gikuyu, Masai and Kalenjin. Furthermore, few Gikuyu attended in the earlier years because the launching of the Bible School coincided with the murder of Miss Stumpf and the crises over female circumcision. Though the Luo did have their own vernacular Bible School for some years, it did not continue long because of the limited number of A.I.C. Luo students who attended. Kapsabet Bible School was not begun until 1954 and then it was conducted in Kiswahili.

The universal conviction of the older missionaries and the Akamba with whom I spoke, is that the strength of the A.I.C. among the Akamba is due to the Akamba trained in their vernacular tongue, using their own vernacular Bible for a long period of time since 1928. The truth of the Word of God was able to penetrate the hearts of the people more effectively because it was communicated in their own mother tongue.

Barrett stresses the strength and power found in the vernacular Bible translations. "Vernacular Scriptures have far greater power to communicate and create religious dynamic than versions in lingua franca such as Swahili…" The vernacular translation enables the people group to grasp the inner meanings of such profound and intricate biblical doctrines. "The vernacular translation, if it were made, would enable the tribe to understand the deepest mysteries of the Kingdom of God…" (Barrett 1968:133)

As these evangelists and pastors, trained in the Word of God, proclaimed the Gospel and called people to repentance and faith in Christ, there was of necessity oral theology. They reflected on God's revelation in their vernacular Bibles. They sought to communicate the meaning of that divine Word in relevant and effective ways. The gradual growth in the churches reflects the fact that the truth and meaning of God's Word was understood and believed.

We can affirm, therefore, that African Christian Theology is not of recent origins but began to be developed from the very beginning of the Christian Church in Africa. For the Gospel appeared to be relevant to the needs of the African peoples.

## Reasons for the Contemporary Developments

Nevertheless, even though some basic steps had been taken from the beginning of the African Church to express the Christian faith in African terms, certain problems prevailed in the interpretation and application of biblical revelation. These problems were felt at times by some missionaries. But the real concern for making the Christian faith more fully relevant to Africa awaited the rise of national leadership in those churches which gained independence from the founding missions and churches. This all coincided with the pan-African movement toward political independence and freedom after World War II.

**Confusion of Gospel and Culture:** A major problem during the colonial era and widely recognized today was the popular equation of Christianity with western civilization. Western culture was thought to be the embodiment of Christian values. During the first half of this century missionaries easily contrasted "the dark continent" with their "Christian homelands."

Complicating the problem was the relationship of the missionaries to the colonial masters. By their race, nationality, culture and religion the missionaries were identified with the colonial masters in the eyes of the African population. Regardless of the many differences, and even regardless of the hostilities between the missionaries and the colonial powers, there was an inevitable cultural bond that drew the missionaries to the friendship of the colonialist. And the African recognized this. The missionaries together with the colonizers, all from "the enlightened West," were seeking to uplift the African population from their "primitive" life.

"In line with the general outlook of the times, even in religiously indifferent matters, Western cultural patterns were rated far superior to African ones and were accordingly insisted upon within the church." (Baeta 1964:20) Thus culture and the Gospel were confused.

In Kenya the Alliance of Missionary Societies appointed the Native Customs Board to consider various African customs. One such issue was dowry. Even though the patriarchs in the Old Testament paid dowry for their wives (eg. Gen. 24:59, 61; 29:24), this African custom did not find favour because it was strange by western standards. After making a study of the matter, The Native Customs Board reported back to the Alliance in January 1919. They agreed that the Societies should urge the African Church Councils to teach their converts not to demand dowry in the marriage of their daughters. But they felt it was impractical to require baptized bachelors not to pay more than a certain maximum as dowry. In the end "the ultimate disappearance of the dowry be looked for more as a result of Christian teaching than government prohibition or regulations."

Some years later in a strange reversal, the Church of Scotland Mission and the Africa Inland Mission actually required that half of the bride price be paid before any marriage. Marriage of communicants before half the bride price was paid constituted grounds for church discipline (Barlow 1925).

When western culture (or any culture for that matter) becomes so confused with the Gospel that judgments are made on the basis of that foreign culture, inevitable problems arise. When Christians in the West contrast their "western empires" with "savage tribes," can we wonder that many of these cultural presuppositions of westerners are now being challenged?

The fact is that the whole colonial mentality prior to African independence was that of missionaries from "Christian nations" taking the gospel to peoples and nations living in total darkness. It was all too easy for the missionary to confuse his own cultural values with the supra-cultural values of Scripture. As Dickson observed, "In the early days of missions in Africa no clear distinction was drawn between the gospel and Christianity." (1974:199) "And Christianity, as it was brought to Africa, was the gospel together with a cultural encrustment of a Western nature." (Dickson 1974:199)

**Rejection of African Culture:** The counterpart of this problem was that missionaries found it all too easy to reject African beliefs and practices without adequate understanding. "Ignorance of the real facts created many false images of Africa, and inadequate observations often led to exaggerations. Religion was one of the aspects of African life which suffered from misunderstanding and distortions." (Hassing 1971:510) As a result, Fashole-Luke complains that, "African religious customs, rites, practices, and beliefs were rejected without being properly evaluated." (Fashole-Luke 1974a:97)

Dietrich Westermann, a western missionary, wrote, "The Africans have been treated by us as having no religion, no language, no traditions, no institutions, no racial character of their own, as empty vessels to be filled with European or American food." (Goreham 1975:233)

In many ways Fashole-Luke and Westermann seem unduly harsh, though they are representative of most contemporary scholarship on the subject. Their opinion certainly does not reflect the assessment made by the older missionaries themselves. The older A.I.M. missionaries were renowned for their mastery of the vernacular language. Some of these like Linnell Davis, Ken and Herb Downing, Earl Anderson, George Rhoad, Paul, Eric and Bill Barnett learned the language while growing up in Kenya as missionary children. They learned by listening, observing and doing. Furthermore up until the 1940's the language policy of the Africa Inland Mission required mastery of the vernacular, not Kiswahili.

Thus for instance C.F. Johnston with a mastery of Kikamba would sit with the elders at the **thome** and talk with them for hours. Some of these missionaries are renowned for their skill and mastery of the vernacular, knowing the older and deeper vocabulary better than the younger generations of Africans. Would not this knowledge of African languages enable them to penetrate with understanding the African customs and culture?

When talking to these older missionaries, it becomes quite apparent that they understood and valued many of the traditional ways of the Africans. To say that the A.I.M. was negative on all the African customs and culture as some scholars maintain is quite inadmissible. Various aspects of African culture which they appreciated include family cohesiveness where the child always belongs and is accepted; respect for the elders; decorum and self-restraint; feeling of mutual responsibility; decency in dress, speech and behaviour; social security for the aged in their own homes; hospitality was so genuine that people never prepared much food for a journey; fraternity and communal relationships were so strong that they cared for one another; apart from severe famines, people never died of poverty for the food was shared; family solidarity was so strong that divorce was rare and orphanages unnecessary; crime was limited, nothing like it is today.

Yet it is illuminating to talk with the Africans who knew and appreciated some of these missionaries, Africans who until this day love and respect those missionaries. From their perspective these missionaries only had a superficial knowledge of African customs and culture, depending upon the Christian African to explain the meaning. One of the earliest converts in Machakos observed, "It

31

seemed that missionaries saw so much darkness in the old days, that they did not seek advice. Only today when there is light do missionaries seek advice."

There is reason to believe that many missionaries avoided certain African traditions and did not research them. We know that today the older African Christians have separated themselves from their traditional culture, to the point that anyone observing a dance or learning from a medicine man is suspect. From this approach we might infer that the early missionaries did likewise.

In fact missionary testimony supports this inference. One veteran missionary who himself was "a missionary kid," doubts that the early missionaries ever consulted with the Africans on the meaning of their culture. Missionaries therefore, frequently misjudged the meaning of the culture because they did not take time to investigate and learn, according to this veteran missionary.

This missionary returned to Kenya at the age of 24. Whenever he drove down the road and passed a group of Africans dancing, he would turn his head the other way. The belief of the African Christians in those days was that anyone who stopped and observed was opening himself up to temptations. The Christian elders admonished Christians not to watch the dances.

On the one hand, we could argue that every missionary must learn the culture from the nationals. He should seek to understand the peoples with empathy. How can we learn without sympathetic listening? How can we learn the meaning of a people's world view without penetrating research which surely includes observation and listening?

On the other hand, those missionaries were struggling to establish a Christian church among a peoples who rejected Jesus Christ. What these early A.I.M. missionaries did was similar to the practice of the early Christian Church, struggling to plant a Christian witness in the midst of European paganism.

We read in the **Teaching of the Twelve Apostles,** "My son, flee from all wickedness and from everything like it...My child, do not be an observer of omens, for this leads to idolatry; or engage in witchcraft, astrology or ritual ablutions. Do not even desire to see these things (or hear them), for from all these idolatry is born." (Schopp 1947:173) To avoid the temptation of returning to sinful practices, both African believers and the missionaries advocated separation from and avoidance of all such traditional practices, in much the same way as that which was advocated by missionaries who sought to plant the church among European pagans in early church history.

Whatever one's perspective of the missionary era may be, one fact is undeniable. African customs and beliefs were not adequately addressed by the Word of God. Little theological reflection was done on how the Gospel related to traditional culture, except to reject various customs. The colonial mentality did not encourage mutual theological reflection by both missionaries and national believers. Thus African culture was not penetrated by the Word of Jesus Christ. And missionaries to a distressing extent were influenced by their own cultural perceptions derived from their western nations of origin instead of from the biblical world view.

32

## Example of Sickness

A case in point is the Christian approach to sickness. One of the greatest reasons for African converts turning back to traditional religion is illness. In traditional African culture there was high mortality. Sickness frequently led to death. Because sickness is often not understood and because it frequently leads to death, African believers sometimes become very frightened at the prospect of illness.

To the medicine man the people traditionally turned for assistance. He was always there to help. Illness was never explained solely through natural means. There were reasons behind every illness that were rooted in their religious world view. The cure generally required more than natural herbs. Treatment included help from the spiritual world in dealing with the spiritual causes of the illness.

With the coming of the missionaries two developments took place. Western medicine was introduced in dispensaries and hospitals with a natural explanation for all sickness and healing. Secondly, many missionaries treated former diagnoses of sickness, as superstition, unworthy of belief. Whether these messengers of the Christian Faith were conscious of the problem or not, they were presenting a western approach to the sickness and healing which minimizes the centrality of the supernatural in all healing. Sickness is caused by microscopic organisms and the sick will become well through natural medications - yes, and through prayer.

Now we are well aware of the tremendous spiritual impact medical care has had upon the African peoples in bringing them to a knowledge of Jesus Christ. Hospitals and dispensaries sponsored by evangelicals have always integrated to some extent the spiritual aspect of life with physical healing. But the integration has been inadequate. Sometimes the doctors and nurses are over worked and feel unable to devote extra time to patients with spiritual needs. Or the spiritual needs are thought of in terms of receiving Christ as Lord and Saviour.

Many an African believer is willing to receive treatment from western style dispensaries, hoping for a cure. But whenever they are not healed, they do what most people do, namely, seek help from other sources. But in Africa those sources are Traditional Religion and the medicine man. And sickness is one of the greatest causes for African believers to return to the medicine man who communicates with the spirit world.

The Gospel simply has not penetrated the soul of Africa because the heart of Africa was not seriously reflected upon from the Christian view point. What does God have to say to people immersed in the African traditional world view where sickness is always the result of malignant personal agents? We need a biblical theology of divine healing within the African context.

## Example of Spirit Possession

Another case in point is spirit possession. It appears that many missionaries failed to take spirit possession seriously with a biblical world view. Instead of acknowledging the reality of spirit possession and seeking God's remedy, remembering the ministry of our Lord, spirit possession was treated by many as superstition. The natural world view of the West overwhelmed the biblical world view for

33

many a missionary. Consequently, the reality of the supernatural powers of the Evil One was dismissed as manifested in witchcraft and sorcery and in communication with the dead.

An interesting experience in a particular church is relevant here. The pastor, an esteemed, elderly leader in the church, was preaching. In the course of his sermon he denied the reality of witchcraft, calling it, mere superstition. Suddenly, a woman stood up in the church and rebuked him. She had recently been converted from a life of involvement in traditional witchcraft. Contrary to the opinion of the pastor, she steadfastly maintained that witchcraft was not mere superstition. There was a spiritual reality behind that traditional practice.

Enough cases of this sort have come to my attention to persuade me that in fact this is the approach taken by many an older missionary. Consequently, the churches are unable to deal with this common African problem, spirit possession. By denial rather than power encounter they seek to deal with possession. And when some younger student pastors seek to exorcise the evil spirits in the Name of Jesus Christ, they are looked upon as radicals who have departed from the faith.

In my own experience I find that we are all strongly influenced by the world view of those cultures from where we have come. Africans, brought up in a world view saturated with the supernatural, are inclined to interpret events by a supernatural explanation far more than the westerners. And missionaries from the West, yes, evangelical missionaries who accept the complete authority of the Scriptures, are more inclined to find a natural explanation in a given event.

Now what we have been saying is this. Given all the dynamics of the colonial era, the African perspective on theology was not seriously studied. Western culture was confused with the Gospel. African culture was frequently rejected without fully understanding the meaning through adequate research. Consequently, the Word of God has not penetrated African culture to the inner core.

## A Theology of Relevance

The bottom line of this whole colonial mentality was that the Gospel was not preached with as much relevancy as it deserved. Baptized Christians and "marginal Christians" did not always "feel at home" in the institutional church planted by the missionaries with its foreign hymns and formal liturgy. Nor have their spiritual needs been met because the Gospel has not been applied to those areas where they hurt and where they have need. Christians lived "split-level" lives. One level was Christian and the other level was traditional. The African Christian "suffered from a form of religious schizophrenia. With part of himself he has been compelled to pay lip service to Christianity as understood, expressed and preached by the white man. But with an ever greater part of himself, a part he has been often ashamed to acknowledge openly and which he has struggled to repress, he has felt that his Africanness was being violated." (Tutu 1978:366)

Arising out of all this has been the need to africanize theology. That is, there is a need to relate biblical revelation to African culture. There is a need to answer the questions which the Africans are asking. Instead of having a monologue, the

34

teacher instructing the peoples what he thinks the questions and answers are, we need dialogue in order to discover from the African believers themselves a better understanding of their felt needs. And then together we search the Scriptures and reflect upon God's revelation in the African context.

African Christian Theology is a call to meet the felt needs of the Africans in an African manner according to the Scriptures. African Christian Theology is a call to communicate the eternal Gospel in the form and idiom which the people can best understand. African Christian Theology's underlying concern will always be to so interpret the gospel that it can really be heard and lived in the African setting. "The African theologian's task is to understand the modern African and his past and relate the Gospel to him and his needs." (Gelzer 1970:1092)

Perhaps that is the crux of the need for African Christian Theology, "to understand the modern African and his past and relate the gospel to him and his needs." On one level, africanizing Christianity involves the contextualizing of her worship and witness. This includes contextualizing the African churches' hymnody, musical instruments, liturgy, vestments and architecture. Worship must involve the whole inner being. What stirs the westerner's soul is quite different from what stirs the African's soul. Anything in our "worship services" which hinders true worship from the heart should be removed in favour of that which is more relevant. There are very few western hymns sung in our churches which stir the heart like those written locally. And the beat of those western hymns which are readily accepted in Africa is quite different from the stately hymns of the faith from the West. African Christian Theology must think its way through the whole biblical teaching of worship in the African context.

But at a deeper level, African Christian Theology must touch the world view of the traditional African, meeting the African where he is.

To root the Gospel in African soil has many implications. There must be a significant degree of cultural continuity. By cultural continuity we refer to the fact that in many ways Christianity must incorporate the fine and noble aspects of a given culture if Christianity is to become truly indigenous. There must be a sense that this is African Christianity and not merely a Christianity transported from the West.

Many African theologians (cf. Fashole-Luke 1974a:98) recognize that there must be "aspects of discontinuity between the Gospel and any culture," and that this discontinuity may be ignored in "ethnic theologies." That is, there are parts of any culture which must be abandoned by Christians because it falls under the judgment of God. If the Gospel is domesticated by being unduly accommodated to the culture, it will lose the authority of the Word of God. If the Gospel is accommodated to a culture through compromise of the fundamental aspects of biblical teaching, then that gospel parts company with the Gospel of Jesus Christ.

However, "Christianity always comes with a cultural conditioning, but what those engaged in the task of producing an African Christian Theology are claiming, is that this 'cultural conditioning' must be African and not Western. Furthermore, it is being argued that African Christians must produce a Theology which bears the distinctive stamp of African thinking and reflection." (Fashole-Luke 1974a:98) African Christian Theology "involves steeping oneself in the patterns of thought of traditional African religions and studying Christianity in the light of that heritage, thus endeavouring to find points of contact between African traditional beliefs and Christian beliefs, so that Christianity can be more effectively and relevantly proclaimed to the African situation." (Fashole-Luke 1974a:100) This study of traditional religion is to be "positive" and not "negative," according to Fashole-Luke, as has been the tendency in the past.

Cultural continuity includes the relating of the Gospel to African Traditional Religion. Many anthropologists had predicted that belief in witchcraft and sorcery would disappear with the development of education. Missionaries had forecast the gradual decline of traditional religion. But to the dismay of many, the traditional practices have had a grip on many professing Christians in times of personal crisis. "The African religion has not disappeared; it is being revived." (Hassing 1971:512) African Theology seeks to relate biblical revelation to African traditional culture and religion.

## A Theology of Self-hood

African Christian Theology is also related to the African's assertion of his own "Africanness." In reaction to the negative feelings toward himself and his culture which he imbibed from the colonial era, the African theologian seems to reassert his own dignity and self-worth. Recent developments in African Christian Theology cannot be understood apart from the historical context of oppression through the slave trade and European colonization. In the 1930's there was an awakening of African consciousness. L.S. Senghor advocated Negritude, a pride in the rediscovery of African culture, religion and language. African Christian Theology is a quest for African self identity.

African Christian Theology, as it is developing, might be considered as a theology of selfhood, not only in recognition of the changed status of much of Africa, from the colonial to the post-colonial period, but also as a symbol of the desire of the Church in Africa to be in a position to present Christ as one who knows and understands the hopes and fears of Africans... (Dickson 1975:45)

"The focal point of African theology would remain the same: an expression of the Christian faith which does justice to the African's humanity and God-given ways of life and thought." (Dickson 1975:45)

African Christian Theology is in many ways a reactionary theology. In the process of asserting one's own self-worth and making a distinctive contribution to theology, there is a tendency toward reaction against what has been taught them by the missionaries prior to independence. As Desmond Tutu declares, "Most of what is subsumed under the heading 'African Theology' is the result of reaction against cultural and ecclesiastical colonialism." (Tutu 1978:364) Much time is devoted to the criticism of past missionaries and missions for their failures. Attempts

36

are made to construct a new theology based on a new methodology which is distinctive from all other past theologies.

The dynamics of cultural dissimilation are well known. People, wanting to be different, assert their uniqueness by different means. A church which desires to assert her own uniqueness may do so by developing distinctive differences in her theological beliefs or church practices. Cultural dissimilation has been used to explain the theological differences which have surfaced in the history of the Christian Church. No doubt this process is at work many times through the development of African Christian Theology.

Baeta, more than 20 years ago at the time when Africa was gaining independence, commented that "The present reaction, usually referred to as the African Cultural Renaissance, is therefore bound to confront the churches with a number of problems." (1964:20) Customs are restored to respectability, such as the pouring of libations in Ghana, "not necessarily because its original religious value is still acknowledged or believed in, but rather because it is the genuinely African framework for saying prayers and for otherwise communing with the supernatural world." (Baeta 1964:20)

As the African peoples have thrown off the political yoke of colonialism, as they are now seeking to deal with the economic yoke of neo-colonialism, so the Christian Church is seeking to deal with the ecclesiastical yoke of missionary Christianity. It is reactionary but it can also be positive. As Fashole-Luke has said, "African Christians must produce a Theology which bears the distinctive stamp of African thinking and reflection." (1974a:97) While the African Christians react to those trappings which appear to them foreign and non-African, they have the obligation with all Christians to understand what God is saying through the Scriptures in order to make the Christian faith their own faith.

## Conclusion

The recent development of African Christian Theology, then, is a mark of maturity in the African Church.

> African Christian theologians rightly feel that, so far, they have lived a theology which they have not reflected on by themselves, but which the missionaries thought for them and brought ready baked from their homes. Having become mature, African Christian theologians legitimately aspire to rethink theology for themselves. (Daidanso 1983:66)

We may say then, that the "transplanted theology" which lacked total relevancy for the Africans was the gunpowder that exploded. The fire which ignited the gunpowder was the movement toward independence. World War II quickened the pressure for independence. Only after World War II did significant numbers of Africans undertake advanced theological study overseas. As they returned to their home churches in the 1950's, many churches then in the process of receiving independence from their founding missions, these young educated leaders began "to examine their inherited theology in the light of the present and to begin reformulating their thinking in the setting of their own culture." (Gelzer

1970:1091) "African theology - in the sense of theology 'done' by Africans - is relatively new. Indeed African theologians as a recognizable professional group did not exist until rather recently." (Gelzer 1970:1091)

# A SURVEY OF THE LITERATURE

Having observed some of the features of African Christian Theology and the need which gave rise to this theological development in Africa, we now turn to a brief survey of the literature on the subject during the first 30 years. We begin in the post World War II era when African nations and churches were moving toward independence. Both missionaries and national Christians began thinking anew of the relationship between the Gospel and African culture. The catchword at that time was "indigenization."

In May 1955 a Conference was held in Accra, Gold Coast, sponsored by the Christian Council. The topic of discussion was "Christianity and African Culture." (Christian Council 1955) Eight lectures were presented by theologians, churchmen and sociologists, both African and missionary. Professor Busia stated the importance of the Conference in a few words. "For conversion to the Christian Faith to be more than superficial, the Christian Church must come to grips with traditional beliefs and practices, and with the world-view that these beliefs and practices imply." (1955:iii) Various topics of the African world view were discussed from a Christian perspective. Unfortunately, the perspective was only a generally (though genuine) Christian perspective, without any attempt to search the Scriptures and come up with a theology of African culture. This tragic lack of biblical study in the 1950's has become the unfortunate hall mark of most conferences and consultations on African Christian Theology since that time.

In 1960 Bengt Sundkler, a Lutheran missionary to South Africa, wrote a book entitled, **The Christian Ministry in Africa** (1960). One chapter of the book treated the topic, "Towards Christian Theology in Africa." Sundkler stressed the need for relevancy, interpreting Christ in terms of the African experience. Theology as translation is an "ever-renewed reinterpretation to new generations." (1960:281)

Sundkler's book stimulated others to think along similar lines. Harry Sawyerr, a Canon in the Anglican Church in Sierra Leone and Professor of Theology in Fourah Bay College, Sierra Leone, wrote a response to Sundkler, expressing gratitude for Sundkler's "lucid and precise" presentation (1963). Interestingly enough, Sawyerr wonders whether Sundkler has overrated the African myths by calling them "original revelation" and thereby minimizing the Old Testament. This is one of several examples where African theologians have tended to be more conservative than their missionary colleagues. Sawyerr proceeded to suggest several lines of approach to theology for Africa, "based on the life setting and thought-world of the African." (1963:269)

The following year in 1964, Professor C.G. Baeta of the University of Ghana, stated that one of the two most important issues facing the Younger Churches is "the relation of Christian faith to local cultures and how the Younger

Churches may achieve a distinctive self-hood of their own." (1964:19) Baeta speaks of African Christian Theology in terms of its relevancy, effectiveness and indigeneity.

In 1965 the All Africa Conference of Churches co-sponsored with the Theological Education Fund (TEF) a Theological Consultation at Ibadan. These papers were eventually printed in book form, published in 1969 (Dickson and Ellingworth 1969). This book contains eight papers by Africans on belief in sacrifices, priesthood, man, ethics, vital participation and the spirit world. The consultation reflects deep interest in African beliefs, but fails to interact with the Scripture. The one exception is the article written by John Mbiti on Eschatology (1969:159-184).

In 1966 Donald Jacobs, a Mennonite missionary in Tanzania with his Ph.D. earned through the studying of the Akamba, mimeographed a course on theology for private circulation (Jacobs 1966). This is a reasonable effort on the part of an evangelical Christian theologian in Africa to deal with African questions in a course on theology. In the preface Jacobs wrote, "I became aware of some of the great blind spots while teaching Theology in Africa...the Church in the West has simply not tried to answer questions which it has not first asked." (Preface) This is an experimental effort on the part of a missionary to make theology more relevant for Africa.

In 1968 the venerable professor of theology in Fourah Bay College, Sierra Leone, Harry Sawyerr, made a major contribution in his book entitled, **Creative Evangelism.** In the book the author wrestles with a new Christian encounter with Africa, seeking fresh approaches in doctrine and liturgy. Canon Sawyerr repudiates that historic Christianity which holds that "the Bible is infallibly authoritative." (1968:69).In this he becomes representative of many theologians in Africa today.

In 1969 The Lutheran World Fellowship's Department of Theology sponsored a theological consultation which convened at their Lutheran seminary in Makumira, Tanzania (Peterson 1970).Theologians from nine African countries and many different denominations met. They spoke of "Christian Theology in Africa Today," reflecting both a reserve for the term, "African Theology," and the lack of popular usage of that label. They sensed an urgent need for more African theologians since two-thirds of the theologians present were expatriates.

In 1970 David Gelzer, a member of a theological faculty in the Cameroons, defined "Africa theology in the sense of theology 'done' by the Africans." (1970) At the time Gelzer did not believe there was any consensus as to what African Theology is. But he saw the task of the African theologian as "bridge-building." Raimo Harjula read a paper at a Religious Workshop entitled, "Towards a Theologia Africana" (1970).

Another Westerner, Per Hassing, Professor of World Christianity at Boston University School of Theology, spoke of the need "to struggle more seriously than ever before with the problems and questions emerging from African life."

(1971) Indigenization will become a reality only as Christians address the questions "arising out of Africa's long past."(1971:513)

From a totally different perspective, Diginga wa Said who lived under Belgian colonialism for 20 years, writes of the need to decolonize theology (1971). "White theology" was used by the colonialist, he maintains, to enslave Africans and instil a feeling of inferiority into the blacks. Hence the African Church needs to be decolonized just as African nations were politically decolonized.

Sawyerr in the same year wrestled with the problem, "What is African theology?" (1971) He is somewhat troubled with the word, "African." While he recognizes that Africans understand the culture of the soil on which they are nurtured better than most foreigners would" (1971:17), he also deplores any attempt to define Theologia Africana "As specifically devised and produced for Africans per se." (1971:22) He prefers to adopt the suggestion "that the term 'African' is primarily a mythological term, expressive of love for a continent or commitment to an ideal." (1971:23) Sawyerr concludes by saying, "In spite of the difficulties inherent in the term Africa, there is a strong case for A Theologia Africana which will seek to interpret Christ to the African in such a way that he feels at home in the new faith." (1971:24)

In 1971 John Mbiti published the first, lengthy treatise on African Christian Theology (1971). Though it contains both ethnological and theological errors (see later discussion), the book represents the most scholarly example of someone trying to examine Scripture in the context of Africa.

Again in 1971 another book was produced on African Christian Theology, this time by a Roman Catholic (Nyamiti 1971). This small book of 50 pages is a complex mixture of worthwhile observations, traditional Roman Catholicism and a critical view of Scripture.

"Theology in Africa" began in the 1960's. Not until 1971 did African Christian Theology come of age with a greater frequency in the use of the expression. The year 1971 was significant in that the greatest number and most significant contributions to date were published in that year. One might say that the need for African Christian Theology is rooted in the African Christian Church from the earliest years. The post-World War II years which brought independence to Africa saw a greater interest and respect for traditional culture. Christians, living in this nationalistic context, began to relate their Christian faith more and more to their traditional culture which is permeated by African Traditional Religion. By 1971 the movement toward African Christian Theology became a tide, with more significant contributions published than all other previous years combined.

Thereafter, the tide evolved into a flood of contributions on the subject of African Christian Theology. In 1972 more articles were written and more conferences were held (Rubingh 1972; Agbeti 1972; McVeigh 1972). Two conferences were held in East Africa on Black Theology and African Christian Theology (Mshana 1972). The Conference of Black Churchmen sponsored by the African Commission of the National Committee of Black Churchmen in the United States was held in Dar es Salaam, Tanzania, in August 1971. They accepted no white participants on the basis that "If you're white, you can have no way of knowing what it is to be black." (Mshana 1972:20) The major thrust of the conference was the need for black people to re-educate themselves in order to understand themselves, and to communicate creatively with Blacks in Africa and elsewhere.

In January 1972 The Theological Consultation in African Theology and Church Life was sponsored by the Department of Religious Studies and Philosophy of Makerere University and held in Makerere University. Their concern was the development of a relevant theology for Africa. African Christian Theology emerges from the life, culture, traditions and faith of the African peoples.

In 1973 an even greater flood of articles and consultations dealt with African Christian Theology (Buthelezi 1973a, 1973b; Dickson 1973; Mbiti 1973; Thomas 1973). A consultation was held at the Lutheran Theological College in Natal, South Africa, in September (Becken 1972). This consultation reflects South African Christian Theology of the early 1970's and consists of many smaller papers delivered by many different theologians.

In 1974 further steps were taken to clarify what African Christian Theology really is and why it is needed (Fashole-Luke 1974a; Dickson 1974; Mbiti 1974a). Fashole-Luke developed one of the themes of African Christian Theology, namely, ancestors, and attempted to baptize this traditional element into the Christian Church (1974b). In that same year "An Institute on Ancestor Veneration and the Communion of Saints" was sponsored by the Association of Theological Institutions in East Africa in Nairobi, Kenya.

In the year 1975 further efforts were made at clarifying what African Christian Theology is and relating this to Black Theology of South Africa (Glasswell 1975; Goreham 1975; Kurewa 1975; Long 1975; Tutu 1975). Kwesi Dickson wrote a significant article on the importance of developing a methodology for a proper development of African Theology (Dickson 1975). The year 1975 is also important for it marks the first major contribution by an evangelical African, with the publication of **Theological Pitfalls in Africa** by Byang Kato (1975a). Aylward Shorter, a Roman Catholic priest and lecturer at Makerere University, wrote a significant book entitled **African Christian Theology** which seeks "to show how African Christian Theology must grow out of a dialogue between Christianity and the theologies of African Traditional Religion." (1975:1)

In 1976 a miscellaneous assortment of articles was published. The late Byang Kato published an article on "Theological Issues in Africa"(1976). John Mbiti wrote an article expressing the need for a greater emphasis on the Bible in African Christian Theology (1976). A book was published containing a collection of brief articles on third world theologies (Anderson 1976) which includes the discourse on "The Quest for African Christian Theologies" by Fashole-Luke (Anderson 1976:135-150). Lymo develops "a theology of Ujamaa socialism in Tanzania." (1976) Eugene Uzukwu wrote the article entitled, "Notes on Methodology for an African Theology" (1977). In August 1976 the Ecumenical Dialogue of Third

World Theologians was held in Dar es Salaam, Tanzania. The papers presented at the conference are published in **The Emergent Gospel** (Torres 1978).

In 1977 a couple of other consultations were held on African Christian Theology which resulted in publications. The All Africa Lutheran Consultation was held in Botswana in February 1977. This laid the foundation for the All Africa Lutheran Consultation on Theology in the African Context held the following year, October 1978, in Baborone, Botswana. In preparation for the Baborone Conference they compiled and mimeographed **Background Materials** (Bares 1978a, 1978b), mostly taken from the papers read in the Pan African Conference of Third World Theologians held in Accra, Ghana, December 17-23, 1977. The papers from the Pan African Conference were eventually published under the title, **African Theology En Route** (Appiah-Kubi 1976). Apart from the papers prepared for these conferences, nothing else was published on African Christian Theology, demonstrating the crucial role that conferences and consultations have played in the development of African Christian Theology.

In 1978 and the years following, brief articles continued to be written which reflect the provisional and tentative nature of African Christian Theology after 30 years of discussion (Lundblad 1978; Kanyandago 1978; Tutu 1978; Goba 1979, Kinney 1979; Lugira 1979; Roberts 1978-79; Setiloane 1980; Fashole-Luke 1981). In 1979 a significant contribution was made by J.Pobee in his book, **Towards an African Theology.** Another helpful monograph was published in 1983 by Osadolor Imasogie entitled, **Guidelines for Christian Theology for Africa.** Defense of a contextualized theology for Africa is based on the fact that the Christian faith is an incarnational religion and the fact that the quasi-scientific world view of western theology is inadequate for the African context.

In 1982 a significant consultation was held in Seoul, Korea. Fifty delegates from the Third World met from August 27 to September 5, 1982, for the Third World Theologian's Consultation. This was an historic moment for this consultation was the first of its kind by evangelicals (Nicholls 1983). Papers were read from Asia, Latin America and Africa on the following topics: Third World Critiques of Western Theology, Third World Critiques of Third World Theologies, Biblical Foundations for Evangelical Theology in the Third World, and Towards an Evangelical Theology in the Third World. Bruce Nicholls who edited and published the articles in one edition of the **Evangelical Review of Theology** commented, "The degree of unity achieved in the midst of incredible diversity and tensions of culture, mission and ecclesiological heritages, economic and political systems is remarkable. It reflects a common determination to uphold the primacy and authority of Scripture and devotion and obedience to one Saviour and Lord." (1983:7)

By 1984 Justin Ukpong in his survey of African theologies (1984) could declare, " 'African Theology' is a household expression today in theological circles all over Africa. Yet, when we get down to defining what it really is, it is sometimes not easy to get a clear answer." (1984:4) He surveys the African theologies under three categories: South African Black Theology, African Liberation Theology and African Inculturation Theology.

While African Christian Theology is as old as the Christian Church in Africa when the Gospel was translated into the mother tongues of Africa, African Christian Theology as an academic discipline is still in her infancy. After some 30 years of initial consultations and discussions we need to move beyond mere reaction to a positive reflection upon God and His will for our lives in the African context and to an exposition of Scripture which gives us understanding of divine truth applied to our own context. As Okeka wrote, "It is merely a waste of paper writing on the failings of the earlier missionaries. Today is our time to put right those things we find undesirable in their missionary methods and practices." (Okeke 1978:49)

But African Christian Theology can only be developed properly through adequate methodology. A faulty methodology will inevitably lead to a faulty theology. Therefore, we turn to the question of methodology being discussed in African Christian Theology.

# *Chapter 3*

# THE METHODOLOGY

The task of thinking through our Christian faith and applying divine truth to our cultural context is both desirable and necessary. But unless a house is built on solid foundations, it will crumble with the passage of time. The house to be built is a Christian theology in Africa. The foundation to be laid is our methodology whereby we develop Christian theology in Africa.

In this chapter we shall first evaluate some aspects of the proposed methodology for theology in Africa. Then some Guidelines will be presented for evangelicals who desire to apply divine revelation to their particular African context.

## A CRITIQUE OF PROPOSED METHODOLOGIES

### Kwesi Dickson

Kwesi Dickson is among the first African theologians who saw the critical need to develop an adequate methodology. In 1974 he made the accurate observation:

> Admittedly, there has been a tendency, in talking of an African Theology, to look at the matter solely from the point of view of the contribution African life and thought can make, and hardly ever from the point of view of biblical revelation...In other words, this quest for an African Theology could proceed on the basis of a faulty methodology, that is, by making a value judgment of certain facets of African life and thought and then seeking sanction from biblical revelation for its incorporation into the expression of the Christian Faith. It seems to us that the reverse is the only valid way to build up a Christian theology...it would be inexcusable to fail to give biblical teaching pride of place in this quest (1974:204).

One year later Dickson wrote an article entitled, "African Theology: Origin, Methodology and Content" (Dickson 1975). In this article he observes that the term, "African Theology," has been in use for the past decade, "but it is only now that the prerequisites for such theology are in the process of being defined." (1975:41) He then mentions three areas where important developments could take place: the church's order of services, study of the Bible and the restatement of basic Christian doctrines.

But the article really fails to come to grips with the methodology by which African Theology is to be done. He does place great emphasis on the primacy of biblical revelation as one relates the Christian faith to African culture. "Indigenization," he says, is a term which makes "a separation between the central revelation of God in Christ, which revelation is unchanging and about which there can be no compromise, and the cultural incidentals of a Western nature which accompanied the Gospel to Africa; the latter must be either discarded or adapted to suit the African traditional culture ethos." (1985:40)

Dickson shows that in the minds of many African theologians, biblical revelation does play an important role. "It is not accidental that the Ibadan consultation had for its theme 'Biblical Revelation and African Beliefs'." (Dickson 1974:204) Elsewhere Dickson declares, "There is the need to make a serious study of the Bible, which, after all, is an indispensable source of theologizing since it reveals what God has done." (Torres 1978:47)

But Dickson also raises our concern about his view of the Scriptures. The study of the Bible has been "woefully neglected by the Church in Africa and .... deserves urgent attention" (1975:42), according to Dickson. Yet he interprets this Bible from the critical point of view which rejects the absolute authority and unity of the Scriptures. "The many hermeneutical tools which scholars have defined over the years are indispensable," Dickson writes, "and in the departments of religious studies all over the continent care is taken to ensure that students are brought up to appreciate the modern critical methods of biblical study." (1975:42)

While evangelical biblical scholars use various hermeneutical tools for the interpretation of Scripture, these tools are all under the authority of the Word of God as we accept the Bible by faith. Faith in Jesus Christ is primary. And Jesus Christ had complete confidence in the Scriptures. Therefore, our faith in Christ compels us to hold to the same faith that He had in the Scriptures. We shall see later on in this book in greater detail what Jesus' attitude was toward the Scriptures. We can merely observe here that His confidence was absolute. "Truly I say to you," Jesus taught, "until heaven and earth pass away, not the smallest letter or stroke shall pass away from the Law, until all is accomplished." (Matt. 5:18)

Dickson has apparently accepted the presupposition of the documentary hypothesis of the Old Testament (1975:43). In this western critical version of the Bible, Moses was not the author of the Pentateuch, the first five books of the Bible. Instead, the critics claim that an editor or several editors compiled the first five books of the Bible from various conflicting sources. In the same way, these critics believe, much of the Bible was compiled through the editing of many contradictory sources. The emphasis in the documentary hypothesis is the faulty, human effort to compile the Bible from various literary sources. By human reason the Scriptures are examined. Man determines what he thinks is true and what is not true.

This critical view of the Bible denies the unity of the Scriptures. The Holy Spirit is not the divine Author. Hence, there are many contradictions in the Bible. Neither are we bound to accept what the Bible teaches. These critics for instance deny that Paul wrote the Pastoral Epistles (I and II Timothy, Titus). Even though these letters claim to be written by the Apostle Paul and even though the Christian Church has over the centuries recognized them as canonical (that is, part of the in-

45

spired Word of God), critical scholars reject Pauline authorship because in their opinion Paul could not have written the letters as they stand.

With these assumptions Dickson opens himself up to serious distortion of what Scripture teaches. The unity of biblical revelation is rejected. When a theologian with these presuppositions takes biblical study seriously, he inevitably wanders from the historic faith of the Christian Church.

This is reflected in a paper Dickson presented in 1977 at the Pan African Conference of Third World Theologians held in Ghana. In his paper on the "Continuity and Discontinuity Between the Old Testament and African Life and Thought" (Bares 1978:39-52), he considers the Old Testament Scriptures. While he maintains that "the exclusivist attitude" in the Old Testament is predominant, another "tradition which, even if it was not the most publicisied, was nevertheless striking for its rejection of an exclusivist attitude to the goyim" (Bares 1978a:42).

Dickson here finds two conflicting teachings in the Bible. In most places you find "the exclusivist attitude," holding to an exclusive view of revelation and salvation through Israel alone. But Dickson believes that there is another teaching which rejects that "exclusivist attitude." Therefore, we can only conclude that in Dickson's opinion the Holy Spirit is not the One Divine Author of the Bible. Nor is there unity in what the Bible teaches.

Such an approach allows one to pick and choose the "tradition" which is most acceptable to the person reading the Bible. In this particular case Dickson assumes that the Most High God of whom Melchizedek was priest, was the heathen god, Baal, known in Phoenicia (1978:42). Dickson concludes with von Rad, "such a positive, tolerant evaluation of a Canaanite cult outside Israel is unparalleled in the Old Testament" (1978:44).

As evangelicals we cannot escape the inevitable loss and theological consequences of this unorthodox view of Scripture. Dickson notes that at one time the Old Testament was deemed to be very special. "The author of the Old Testament was held to be the Holy Spirit." Dickson acknowledges that, "This kind of attitude did affect the interpretation of the text in so far as it discouraged the raising of questions regarding the limitations of the authors." (Bares 1978a:48)

This frank admission by Dickson must be understood and remembered. As we move along in our study of African Christian Theology we must remember that the major differences between liberal theologians and evangelical theologians is over this very issue. Liberal theologians like Dickson do not believe in the same kind of Bible as evangelicals do. Their view of revelation is different. For this reason their conclusions in African Christian Theology will be radically different. And let us remember that the critical view of the Bible was not first developed in Africa. It was developed in the West and imported into Africa.

For most of church history all Christian theologians held to the view of Scriptures that evangelicals hold to today. They believed that the Bible is the Word of God because the Holy Spirit Himself superintended the writing of every word. As Peter wrote, "for no prophecy was ever made by an act of human will, but men moved by the Holy Spirit spoke from God." (II Pet. 1:21)

46

But with the coming of the Enlightenment in the 18th century, reason was enthroned in the West and took a critical attitude of the Old Testament. The Bible was torn apart and rejected. Instead of the Christian accepting by faith what God had said, he became the judge of what was true and false. Dickson concludes,

> In our time there is a diverse array of tools for studying the Old Testament (and indeed the Bible as a whole), and the influence of various other sciences has been recognized, such as sociology, psychology, and the phenomenology of religion, etc. the employment of these and other tools has resulted in a much broader understanding of the meaning and value of the Old Testament. (Bares 1978a:48)

With this approach to the Scriptures, we need not be surprised by the differing perspectives in African Christian Theology. As Dickson observes, the result is a "much broader understanding of the meaning and value of the Old Testament." The Old Testament (and for that matter, the New Testament) no more has the same weight of authority. We are no longer bound by that meaning and value of the Bible which the Christian Church once held due to the present day liberal belief in the nature of the Bible.

The fundamental reason for some radical opinions in African Christian Theology these days is not that we are taking more seriously the African cultures and religion for the first time. The reason is the radically different view of Scriptures held by many of these theologians. And this radical view of the Scriptures does not have African roots. These theologians like Dickson learned their view of Scriptures from the liberals in western universities and seminaries, either directly or indirectly. Western liberal biblical scholarship has undermined the unity of Scriptures for these theologians. This leads to a broadening of theological options allowed.

As Daidanso writes, "Many of those who speak of African theology take a contrary course. Their tutors are the liberal theologians of Europe. So, under the cover of so-called African theology, is it not liberalism which is subtly finding its way in Africa?" (Daidanso 1983:71)

## Peter Kanyandago

A careful study of all that has been written on African Christian Theology reveals that frequent reference is made to the primary place of divine revelation in the Bible. And yet these authors reflect the same flaws as mentioned above in the writings of Dickson.

Kanyandago at first makes some very commendable statements about the primacy of "the revealed Word." He has been concerned because he receives the impression when reading articles on African Christian Theology "that traditional religions are a kind of another revelation." He then concludes, "However important these religions might be, I think the Christian cannot help subjecting them to the Word of God." This will necessitate "putting aside some of our traditional practices." The whole story of Christianity, whether in Europe, Asia or Africa, "is the story of conversion - turning around, transformation, altering..." (Kanyandago 1978:343)

47

However, he proceeds to undermine everything he has said. He speaks of developing a methodology which puts "revelation and the African culture into a mutual criticism." (1978:343) In concluding his discussion on "the problem of methodology and the epistemological questions," he quotes with apparent approval the words of Maurier. "In my opinion the encounter that an African Theology sets up between the Word of God and African culture, should rather be a **reciprocal interpolation at equal terms** [emphasis mine], putting in question in a mutual criticism the two partners..." (1978:344)

This approach to African Christian Theology will inevitably lead away from historic Christianity, for there is a serious loss of the supreme and final authority of Scripture. The stark contrast between the theology taught by the early evangelists of Africa and what we frequently read of today is not the result of taking the African context more seriously. It is the result of a liberal view of Scripture.

Most of the Christian churches of Africa were founded by evangelicals. But through the past 100 years, liberalism has infested most of the main line Protestant denominations overseas, beginning first with the seminaries and colleges. This low view of Scripture has gradually infiltrated many of the seminaries and theological colleges of Africa from whence this unbelief is filtering down to the local congregations.

Evangelicals have recognized the pitfalls of a low view of Scripture. The Seoul Declaration affirms,

> We have found that some of the presuppositions, sources, and hermeneutics of theologies such as ethnotheologies, syncretistic theologies and liberation theologies are inadequate...We unequivocally uphold the primacy and authority of the Scriptures. For us, to know is to do, to love is to obey. Evangelical Theology must root itself in a life of obedience to the Word of God and submission to the lordship of Jesus Christ. (1983:9)

If there is any such thing as a legitimate African Christian Theology (and there surely is), then obviously, the African culture, worldview and religion must be seriously researched. The importance of such studies looms very large in all the literature on African Christian Theology. The words of Nyamiti express what is said by virtually all other writers on African Christian Theology. "But the lion's share should be allotted to the African religions. Indeed as regards African Theology, the African religions have a specially important role to play." (Nyamiti 1971:18)

We have previously recognized that a study of African Traditional Religion is an essential task. Relevancy is impossible, and contextualization will never be achieved, if we do not seriously relate the Christian faith to the traditional faith of our past. In order to reflect upon God's revelation in our context we must consider both the traditional culture and the contemporary cultural developments. An indigenous African Christianity will take seriously the past and present contexts.

But the basic question in the methodology for developing an African Christian Theology is the relationship between Scripture and traditional religion and culture. At this point there are many reasons for grave concern. Kanyandago speaks of a "reciprocal interpolation at equal terms," making the Word of God one among equals with African traditions. If this is not the intention of Kanyandago, then he is very imprecise.

We have seen that western missionaries confused their culture with the supracultural revelation of Scripture and unfortunately transported western forms of Christianity to Africa. This is to be lamented. But unless we can establish a biblical relationship between Scripture and culture for African Christian Theology, we shall be worse off. Culture will eat up God's revelation. The Word of God will only become a word of God to men in particular historical situations. Though we may allege a certain primacy for the Bible, such claims are only cosmetic.

For evangelicals the Bible must have absolute authority. There can be no "reciprocal interpolation at equal terms" of the Word of God and African culture. What God teaches us in the Bible, and all that the Bible teaches, is God's Word. As such, the Bible is our final authority of what Christians may believe and practice.

## Pan-African Theological Conference

In 1977 the Pan-African Theological Conference, sponsored by the Association of Third World Theologians, was held in Accra, Ghana. About 90 delegates convened from Roman Catholic, Protestant and Orthodox Churches, mostly from Africa. Their Communique reflects this serious confusion in relating Scripture to culture.

On the one hand, they confess that "The Bible is the basic source of African Theology." "No theology can retain its Christian identity apart from the Scripture." (Pan-African Conference 1978:3,5) On the other hand, they suggest other sources for theology. These include: the Christian heritage, African anthropology, African Traditional Religion, including traditional social relationships and contemporary forms of economic, political, social and cultural oppressions.

The basic question is: What is the relationship between the "primary witness of God's revelation in Jesus Christ" and these other sources? They speak of "a critical theology which comes from contact with the Bible, openness to the African realities, and dialogue with non-African theologies." (1978:5) This suggests an interaction between all of these sources of theology with a mere "contact" with Scripture. The Bible is not said to be God's revelation to man but "the primary witness of God's revelation in Jesus Christ." This reflects a neo-orthodox view of revelation. The study of African Traditional Religions is likewise important for they are "a major source for the study of the African experience of God." Such religions can "enrich theology and spirituality." (1978:5) There is found here an unmistakable interchange, a dialogical relationship between the many sources of theology, without any recognition that the Bible is the final source of all authority which judges all else.

49

This Communique reflects the basic outlines of a methodology already being developed for African Christian Theology. These delegates affirmed,

We believe that African theology must be understood in the context of African life and culture and the creative attempt of African peoples to shape a new future that is different from the colonial past and the neo-colonial present. The African situation requires a new theological methodology that is different from the dominant theologies of the West...Our task as theologians is to create a theology that arises, out of, and is accountable to, African people. (1978:6)

If African Christian Theology is not first and foremost accountable to the Word of God, then it ceases to be a biblical theology. If African Christian Theology is primarily accountable to African people, then it becomes an ethnic theology which severs connection with the Church Universal. The Holy Catholic Church, of which all Christians born again by the Holy Spirit are members, has One Head, even Jesus Christ. He Has given us One Holy Spirit who indwells all believers. By His Spirit we are led to One Faith as we reflect upon God's special revelation which is the Bible. As soon as our theology ceases to be apostolic and catholic it ceases to be Christian. By apostolic we mean that our theology is rooted in the teaching of the Apostles. By catholic we mean our theology proclaims universal truth.

For Evangelical Christians, the revelation of God, the Word of God, is the absolute authority in matters of life and faith challenging men and women, habits, customs and cultures of men and of all nations, as well as political, administrative and religious institutions established among peoples. Evangelicals will therefore have a critical attitude toward their cultures, respecting in African habits every thing which is not contrary to biblical faith and rejecting everything that is detrimental to the Word of God... (Daidanso 1983:70)

## J.W. Zvomunondita Kurewa

Kurewa suggests three points in methodology for African Theology: participation, interpretation, and dialogue (Goreham 1975:36-39). The person who does African Christian Theology "fully participates in the African experience(s). This African experience has no formula other than being African or Black." (1975:37) The theologian must participate in the religious community so that he understands "the impressions, judgement, feelings and perceptions of his community both experientially and rationally." (1975:38) He must also hold dialogue with the rest of Christendom, including African theologians and non-African theologians, past and present. "Finally, and above all, African Theology will need constant dialogue with Biblical Theology. Naturally every Christian Theology will have to take the Christian Bible very seriously." (1975:39)

Kurewa is to be commended for the relative primacy which he gives to the Bible. However, several factors are brought to our attention. While he devotes 179 lines to other aspects of his methodology, only 11 lines are devoted to the

Bible. Furthermore, he encourages a dialogue with Scripture which of necessity means give and take, an exchange of ideas. The concept of final authority does not seem to apply to Scripture.

Once again we find that Kurewa, although he approaches the Bible "very seriously," he views Scripture through existential glasses. "Biblical faith" for Kurewa is "a living relationship of the people of God with their God, as it is understood through their testimony in both the Old and New Testaments." (1975:34) These communities of the people of God "testify to the activities of God as they witnessed them." The New Testament communities hold a "very unique position in the whole of Christendom" and therefore "their testimony of faith which they experienced becomes crucially important to all believers in Christ as a basis of dialogue." (1975:34) As they interpreted these events the "humanness of man becomes a crucial factor in theological interpretation. The Jewish and Greek New Testament communities understood God who revealed himself in Jesus Christ with the bias of their own cultural context." (1975:35)

The old liberal view of Scriptures was that the Bible CONTAINED the Word of God. Parts were not inspired. Therefore, some parts of the Bible were in error.

But the more common liberal position today is the neo-orthodox view which seems to be reflected here in the writings of Kurewa. The Bible itself is not the Word of God but it BECOMES the Word of God to us as God speaks to us through the Scriptures. Revelation is always subjective and existential. As soon as the prophets and apostles were confronted with the Word of God in their hearts and tried to record verbally that encounter with God, the record became fallible and full of error. God reveals Himself through His mighty acts as He confronts people with Himself. But God does not communicate verbally. The prophets and apostles in Bible times encountered God through various means. Their human record of these encounters is what we find in the Bible. Because of their place in sacred history, we give these records primacy. They are very important. But they are not final or inerrant or infallible in any sense of the word. They are simply the first among many witnesses. Because in this view, divine revelation is always personal and never verbal. The Bible is the record of man's attempt to record their experiences of revelation. And as Kurewa observes, they are biased. God's revelation is always personal and in the heart, from God to man. This is the existential view of Scriptures as held by a large number of liberals today.

This low view of Scripture is reflected in the vast majority of writings. On the one hand there is a formal acknowledgement that the Bible is to be taken "very seriously." On the other hand, their view of Scripture prevents the Bible from exercising final authority.

According to Kurewa's presupposition, God has revealed Himself through mighty acts. But God apparently has not spoken to give the interpretation of those acts. The meaning of those acts is derived as the communities of the believers reflect on those divine activities. And that reflection is "biased" because of their peculiar cultural contexts. Hence we have diverse theologies in Scripture and, contrasting and contradictory traditions in the Bible. While Kurewa recognizes the "unique position" of the Biblical communities, making their testimony "crucially important to all believers," Karewa has robbed the words of Scripture of divine authority. He does not believe that the Holy Spirit is the Divine Author of the very words of Scripture.

## Desmond Tutu

Is the task of talking about God and His revelation to man "risky business"? When one reads the words of Jesus in the Upper Room, one would hardly conclude that theologizing was "risky" (Jn. 13-17; esp. 14:26; 15:26; 16:12-14). Yet for many theologians there is risk. "In our view," writes Desmond Tutu, "theology is a risky, albeit exhilarating business of reflecting on the experience of a particular Christian community in relation to what God has done, is doing and will do, and the ultimate reference point is the man, Jesus." (Tutu 1978:367)

For theologians who have an existential view of Scripture, the risk is dramatic. The Bible is merely the first among many witnesses to God's revelation, not the final revelation which judges all truth. Scriptures contain many errors, inconsistencies and conflicting interpretations rooted in their differing cultural biases. In the task of contextualizing theology, being faithful to Christian tradition is truly risky. How does one determine what is universally true for all Christians? This is indeed hard to determine when each community of the people of God is left to their own experiential judgment.

Theologians may recognize the need for the guidance of the Holy Spirit. But when the propositional revelation of Scripture is disposed, the Holy Spirit is a mere euphemism for personal opinion. That is, when we deny that the very words of biblical revelation were inspired, then man becomes the judge of what is true and false. There is no authoritative text to which we can turn. In this case each person and each community interprets as he pleases, hopefully led by the Holy Spirit. But there is no objective judge which can help us determine the accuracy of that interpretation. Such an approach to Scripture leads Tutu to conclude, "This means that theology must of necessity be particularistic, existential and provisional. It must glory in its in-built obsolescence...There must then be a plurality of theologies." (Tutu 1978:367) In this case African Christian Theology will be numbered among all those contemporary experiments of theologians in the West who glory in novelty but stray from "the sure word of prophecy."

## Charles Nyamiti

Charles Nyamiti, a Roman Catholic priest from Tanzania, has written on methodology of African Christian Theology (Nyamiti 1971). He speaks of various approaches or methods in the development of African Christian Theology. The Pastoral Approach means that the development of theology should have pastoral motives of loving God and the Church. The "pastoral-minded theologian" will adapt theology to the help of his people so that "there will be no separation between theology and spirituality." (1971:5)

The Apologetical Method in its negative aspect points out the insufficiency and defects of non-Christian religions. But the negative aspect of this method shows "that Christianity answers to, and surpasses, human needs and aspirations." The negative aspect is essential but it "tends to arouse polemic discussions and thus likely to hinder fruitful dialogue." (1971:6) Therefore, the theologian should study the African and Christian themes to find parallels and differences and thereby show how Christianity fulfills the aspirations and needs of the African.

The Pedagogical Method seeks to expound Christian doctrine, solve problems and arrange theological textbooks. Nyamiti takes a typically Roman Catholic approach with great stress on philosophy in general and St. Thomas in particular. When solving problems you begin with the Bible, then consider the Tradition of the Church and then scrutinize the problem "by means of speculation, of which St. Thomas is recommended as the master." (1971:13)

While Nyamiti is constrained by Roman Catholic official doctrine (cf. 1971:1), he appears to have a similar problem as those Protestant scholars mentioned above, in addition to a peculiarly Roman Catholic problem. Church tradition for a Roman Catholic determines the interpretation of Scriptures, for tradition is itself a form of revelation. Nyamiti says, "The African theology will have to search in the sources of revelation (Bible and Tradition) the kernel of Christian teaching...beyond the cultural expressions through which it is conveyed." (1971:22) In practice, then, church tradition for Roman Catholics is the binding authority as to what African theologians should believe. For he defines African Christian Theology as "the very self-same Catholic doctrine expressed and presented in accordance with the African mentality and needs." (1971:1)

But it appears that Nyamiti also has a problem with the authority of Scriptures because of his critical approach to biblical origins. Instead of accepting the plain teaching of the Scriptures, he allows contemporary culture to determine what is really true or false. For example, he refers to Paul's missionary pastoral method at Corinth, Colossae and Ephesus.

> The Apostle admits without discussion the existence of cosmic personified powers which govern the course of the universe. His Christian originality was to establish an equation between these cosmic forces and the demoniac spirits. The visible phenomena which touch and impress us are due to the invisible beings: the angels of Satan. (1971:22)

Yet according to Nyamiti, this missiological approach of the Apostle was merely an accommodation to the world view of these people. The fact that Paul taught the existence of these spirit beings does not mean that we are bound to believe that they truly exist as spirit beings and objective entities, according to Nyamiti. Saint Paul "does not simply dismiss the 'pagan' beliefs as erroneous, but he takes them at least as symbols useful for Christian demonology." (1971:23) In other words, as we understand Nyamiti, even though Paul teaches the existence of personal spirit beings, he did this only because he accomodated his preaching to the beliefs of the people. Therefore, Nyamiti apparently feels we are not bound to accept what Paul seems to teach.

Once again we are lost in the sea of theological speculation. Contemporary culture, ever changing and diverse, determines what is to be taken as mere "symbols useful for Christians," or what is literally true. If we preach the Gospel to people who believe in literal spirit beings, we may teach about spirits as a useful missiological approach, so as not to offend the people. But if the people to whom we preach do not believe in personal spirit beings, we may take this as merely useful symbolism. It would seem from Nyamiti's discussion that he does not necessarily believe in literal spirits as has been historically believed. But this is not traditional Roman Catholic teaching nor is it African. The Roman Catholic Church has traditionally taught the existence of literal spirits. And we well know that Africans have also done so. This belief of Nyamiti was born out of western rationalism. What is presented as African Christian Theology is merely western rationalism. It is neither African nor biblical.

Nevertheless, he concludes his book with a definitive statement on the primacy of Scripture.

> It is the African culture that has to be transformed to fit the Christian teaching, and not vice versa. It is here that the primary importance of the Bible should be duly taken into account. One should never lose sight of the fact that Sacred Scripture 'ought to be the soul of all theology.' Above all, the theologian should beware of making the Bible a mere instrument for confirming African conceptions and principles, instead of taking it as the starting point and criterion for judging the validity and limits of such conceptions and principles. (1971:27)

We conclude that Nyamiti has a problem of consistency. If he would hold to his convictions as stated above and interpret the Bible accordingly, he would not fall into the error of biblical critics who have a low view of the origins of Scripture.

## John Mbiti

No study on African Christian Theology would be complete without careful consideration given to John Mbiti, "the father" of African Christian Theology. He is easily the most prolific writer in Africa today, having authored many substantial books and hundreds of published articles.

**Sources for African Christian Theology:** Mbiti maintains that there are several sources which contribute toward African Christian Theology, including African religions, African Independent Churches, major traditions of Christendom, biblical theology and the Bible.

From the writings of Mbiti we learn something of the great importance he places in African Traditional Religion and Philosophy. A major part of his scholarly effort is the exposition of African Traditional Religion. He writes on "The Growing Respectability of African Traditional Religion." (1972b:57) He gives lectures on the "Sources for the Study of African Traditional Religions." (1970b) He has written many books on African Traditional Religion, including: **African Religions and Philosophy** (1969); **Introduction to African Religion** (1975a); **African Concepts of God** (1970c); **The Prayers of African Religion** (1975b);

**Akamba Stories** (1966). In many ways he is in the forefront of those who both study and promote the positive investigation of African Traditional Religion which is to serve as the "valuable heritage" to which "Christianity should adapt."

> The old nonsense of looking at African background as devilish, and fit only to be swept away by Euro-American civilization is or should be gone by now...African religious background is not a rotten heap of superstitions, taboos and magic; it has a great deal of value in it. On this valuable heritage, Christianity should adapt itself and not be dependent exclusively on imported goods. (Mbiti 1972a:147)

In Mbiti's opinion African Traditional Religion is a preparation for the Gospel in which Traditional Religion is fulfilled by Christianity. African Traditional Religion is placed on equal footing with the Old Testament as preparation for the coming of Christ.

> When we turn to the New Testament, we find that African religiosity must here assume the listening posture, be at the receiving end, whereas in the area of the Old Testament a certain amount of give-and-take or mutual enlightenment can be carried out. (Mbiti 1972a:172)

Mbiti does not assume that Traditional Religion is without rottenness. He calls on Christianity to "judge and save" African Traditional Religion. "We must give Christianity the opportunity and freedom," Mbiti pleads, "to remove deadness and rottenness from our traditional religiosity." (1972:153) African Traditional Religions are largely but not entirely compatible with Christianity. Traditional Religion can even bring "enrichment" for Christianity in Africa. But this is only after Christianity judges Traditional Religion.

One major source of African Christian Theology according to Mbiti is the Bible. Unlike some African theologians who minimize the Bible in their writtings, John Mbiti is among the forerunners who pleads for greater emphasis on the Scripture.

Among all the papers presented at the 1966 consultation of African theologians in Ibadan, Nigeria (Dickson 1969), Mbiti's paper on Eschatology is the only one which sought to handle biblical revelation as it relates to African beliefs (Dickson 1969:159-184). Mbiti laments, "Very few African theologians are putting their attention on Biblical studies...Only here and there do we have the beginnings of Biblical theology among African scholars." (Mbiti 1976:165)

Showing his concern for the development of genuinely biblical African Christian Theology he has compiled a record of all those published materials and presented them to the Pan-African Conference of Third World Theologians held in Accra, Ghana in 1977. "The Biblical Basis for Present Trends in African Theology" is the title of his paper (Appiah-Kubi 1979:83-94). This paper has been revised and up dated in his more recent publication, **Bible and Theology in African Christianity** (1986:46-63).

Mbiti's concluding remarks show his great concern for biblical studies.

Any viable theology must and should have a biblical basis, and African theology has begun to develop on this foundation. Edward Fashole-Luke is right in reminding us that the Bible is the basic and primary source for the development of 'African Christian Theologies'. Nothing can substitute for the Bible. However much African cultural-religious background may be close to the biblical world, we have to guard against references like 'hitherto unwritten African Old Testament' or sentiments that see a final revelation of God in the African religious heritage. (Appiah-Kubi 1979:90)

Mbiti is to be commended for his admirable sentiments with which he concludes his paper.

As long as African theology keeps close to the Scriptures, it will remain relevant to the life of the church in Africa and it will have lasting links with the theology of the church universal. African theologians must give even more attention to the Bible than is sometimes the case. As long as we keep the Bible close to our minds and our hearts, our theology will be viable, relevant, and of lasting service to the church and glory to the Lord to whom be honor, dominion, and power unto the ages of ages. Amen. (Appiah-Kubi 1979:91)

Further emphasizing the importance of the Bible in African Christian Theology, Mbiti has devoted a whole book to the topic, **Bible and Theology in African Christianity** (1986). He affirms, "Nothing can substitute for the Bible." (1986:59) In surveying the theological literature produced in Africa, he decries the weak emphasis on the Bible.

Generally, scholars have agreed that in the development of a relevant theology for Africa, both biblical revelation and African Traditional Religion are important. Contextualization of the Gospel necessitates serious study of both divine revelation in Scriptures and the African context, the lion's share of the latter being African Traditional Religion. Professor Mbiti has demonstrated genuine concern for both of these focal points.

Mbiti's book, **New Testament Eschatology in an African Background** (Mbiti 1971), reflects his general approach to African Christian Theology. This 210 page New Testament study, in my opinion, is the most scholarly example of relating African traditional beliefs to a study of theology. No other African theologian has made such an extended research.

His first chapter is introductory, giving some historical and enthnographical data concerning the Akamba people, the coming of Christianity into Ukambani and the church planted there. Throughout the book he develops his topic of Eschatology in its various aspects.

The approach in each chapter is fivefold. First, he considers the Akamba traditional concepts related to the topic of eschatology in that chapter. Secondly, he considers the New Testament. Unfortunately, he does not make an inductive study of the Holy Scriptures. Instead, he examines the New Testament through secondary sources of various theologians, "without, however, yielding to the temptation of scrutinizing in detail theories and propositions that scholars are constantly putting forward." (1971:3)

Thirdly, he considers the teaching of "the main evangelizing agent among the Akamba, which is the Africa Inland Mission." (1971:3) Fourthly, he considers how the Akamba Christians understood this Christian teaching brought by the Africa Inland Mission. Finally, Mbiti renders his conclusions and deductions for each chapter.

Mbiti is an example of a Christian theologian who emphasizes the importance of biblical study and who tries to practice what he preaches. Regrettably, however, he did not study the Scriptures directly but through secondary sources of diverse theologians.

His book is filled with Scripture references. Literally, hundreds of Bible references are scattered throughout the entire book, though he nowhere engages in much exegesis of the biblical text. Referring to his article on Eschatology in the book, **Biblical Revelation and African Beliefs** (Dickson 1969), he comments, "however the contents of the book have very little biblical material, except for one essay on eschatology." (Appiah- Kubi 1979:85) Mbiti is quite correct. And the same generalization can be made of most writings which fall under the category of African Christian Theology today. Mbiti has at least tried to deal with the Scriptures.

**Liberal View of Theology:** John Mbiti, however, approaches the Bible through the grid of liberal rationalism. The glasses which he uses to read the Bible are coloured by his liberal view of Scripture. For Mbiti considers the Bible only a "human adviser." He writes, "As far as theology is concerned, let the Bible be our human adviser, and the Holy Spirit our divine adviser." (1986:61).

The great divide between the evangelical and the liberal is their view of Scriptures. Since the evangelical accepts the absolute divine authority of the Bible by faith according to the testimony of Jesus Christ, therefore the Bible becomes the final authority for faith and conduct. But since Mbiti approaches the Scriptures with his liberal presuppositions, he therefore, arrives at liberal conclusions. His presuppositions have a profound bearing on his theologizing. His view of Scriptures determines in a large measure his theological conclusions.

Unfortunately, Professor Mbiti does not engage in biblical exegesis. He does not wrestle with the meaning of our primary source of theology. Instead, as we have stated previously, he studies New Testament Scriptures, not inductively, but through the eyes of theologians who developed their theories of eschatology. He writes of Schweitzer and his "Consistent Eschatology," of Von Dobschutz and his "Transmuted Eschatology," of C.H. Dodd and his "Realized Eschatology," of R. Bultmann and his "Re-interpreted Eschatology," of J.A. Robinson and his "Inaugurated Eschatology," and of Oscar Cullmann. It is of great significance that at no time and in no place does he consider evangelical theologians.

In fact he treats the eschatology taught by the Africa Inland Mission and embraced by the Africa Inland Church as if it were some aberration of historic Christianity, some extreme, unbalanced view of Christian theology. The eschatology of the A.I.M. in its essence is that of historic Christianity and formerly embraced by all the missions which brought the Gospel to Africa. Belief in the second coming of Christ, future judgment and the final state, of either heaven or hell, are found in all the creeds of Christendom, East and West, and from the beginning.

Kato is quite correct when he objects to Mbiti's assertion that the Africa Inland Church is "without theological, doctrinal, historical, liturgical, or ministerial connections with other bodies of the Church universal." Kato contends,

> His criticism is directed, however, against a line of interpretation of which evangelical missions are a part. The Africa Inland Mission (A.I.M.) follows the literal, though not literalistic, interpretation. They take the Word of God on its face value. The A.I.M. has simply passed on to the Africa Inland Church a well established Protestant tradition. (1975:80)

Indeed, it is Mbiti, not the Africa Inland Church, who has lost touch with the biblical teaching of eschatology. Though he never explicitly denies the existence of hell nor does he state categorically that every human being will be saved, he gives the general impression that this in fact is what he believes. Though he never denies that Christ will return again bodily as He went up to heaven, neither does he ever affirm the second coming of Christ as historically taught and believed in the Christian Church.

Instead, he declares that "Jesus may have accepted current notions of Gehenna without necessarily endorcing them all" (1971:66). Indeed, hell is reduced to a mere symbol by Mbiti, for he says, "If people are threatened with being cast into a lake of fire in the next life, the effectiveness of the symbol is largely lost and the Christian Gospel is reduced to negative threats which have no lasting impact upon those who receive or reject Christ." (1971:70) Furthermore, he declares, "The New Testament is explicit that Jesus never promised us a heavenly utopia, but only His own self and His own companionship both in time and beyond, both in space and beyond" (1971:89).

With his sweeping repudiation of the eschatological teaching of the A.I.M, and with the absence of any explicit affirmation by Mbiti that Jesus Christ will return bodily in the future to take His own people to heaven and consign the wicked to eternal damnation, we are compelled to ask some questions. Does Mbiti really believe that Jesus Christ will come in His resurrected body to earth again? Does he really believe that the hope of the Christian today is the blessed return of Christ as taught by the historic Christian Church? Does Mbiti believe that all those whom God has declared righteous by faith will spend eternity with Christ in a place called heaven? Does he believe that there is a hell, a place of eternal retribution for all those who reject the grace of God through Christ?

Instead of affirming the historic Christian truths about the end of this age, he speaks in another vein. "It is almost unthinkable that at the final Resurrection there should be portions of God's creation not involved in the process of presentation, not brought into the conscious presence of God." (1971:172) He suggests that after death "there is almost certainly a spiritual transformation (or 'improvement'), a process of 'perfecting' the souls before the Parousia." (1971:175)

Though he admits this to be speculation, he is hopeful, and procedes to declare: "We venture to speculate that the opportunity to hear or assimilate the effects of the Gospel is continued in the life beyond (cf. 1 Pet. 3:19f), and that death is not a barrier to incorporation into Christ, since nothing can separate 'us' from the love of God (cf. Rom. 8:38)." (1971:175)

After death there may be a period of punishment, but Mbiti finds it "almost impossible to imagine that their punishment will last for all eternity in the same way that Redemption is for eternity." (1971:179) To be "apart from Christ" for one day "is sufficiently tormenting to make the experience of the non-presence of God 'everlasting'." Furthermore, the love of the Father for His erring children "must ultimately win over even the most 'hopeless case' of sinners, and bring home the lost sheep to join the one great fold." (1971:179) Everlasting punishment is therefore reduced by Mbiti to one day. Moreover, "God's love and presence will freely invade that soul (cf. Rom. 8:35, 39) until—let us hope—the soul responds to the Father's embrace and kiss." (1971:180) Thus the "second death" cannot be an absolute reality in Mbiti's opinion (1971:180).

For those in Christ there will be no physical resurrection of the body, Mbiti contends, "for there is no explicit Scriptural warrant to support a materialistic view of the Resurrection body." (1971:172) Furthermore, after some time beyond the grave we shall all loose our individuality so that we cannot recognize our friends as separate individuals. For we will be all in Christ and in one another. "The 'many' will be absorbed into the 'One'."

No doubt we should take seriously the concluding words of Mbiti when he confesses, "The details of what happens beyond the historical plane of human existence are neither for you nor for me to dogmatize about." (1971:180) We all can say with Profesor Mbiti as he states elsewhere, "... for I understand it only in part, since the mysteries of God are inexhaustible." But we are then left bewildered by his dogmatic repudiation of the eschatology of the historic Christian Church. If he cannot dogmatically affirm truths concerning our human existence beyond the Parousia, then how can he dogmatically repudiate the eschatological teaching characteristic of the Christian Church for the past two millennia?

And we are distressed by his repeated dismissal of the futuristic aspect of the Christian hope. Any serious study of the New Testament discloses the importance of this future expectation of the believers. Paul on his missionary journeys never spent a long time in any city where he preached the Gospel. But the blessed hope of the second coming of Christ was apparently part of that Kerygma which he preached everywhere. The Christ Event was the heart of the Gospel, including Christ's birth, crucifixion, resurrection and second coming, even as we find in the Apostle's Creed.

For instance, he spent only a few months in Thessalonica. However, his two epistles make it quite clear that during that short time with them he had expounded concerning "the last things." Various expressions indicate that he had devoted time with them to teach eschatological truth, truth concerning future events. Such expressions include: "For you yourselves know full well..." (1

59

Thess. 5:2); "Do you not remember that while I was still with you, I was telling you these things?" (11 Thess. 2:5)

On the one hand, Paul sought to give the Thessalonian Christians comfort in their future Christian hope because of the serious trials they were presently experiencing as believers. Mbiti contends, "But it is a false spirituality to escape into the Christian world of the hereafter at the expense of being a Christian in the here and now." (1971:60) Though the Apostle Paul taught a lively hope in Christ in the here and now, he repeatedly and specifically held before the suffering Christians the future hope of the Lord's return. Whereas, the non-Christians have no hope (1 Thess. 4:13), the believers can look forward to the return of Christ when both the dead in Christ and the living shall be caught up to be with the Lord forever. Believers are to be encouraged by this future hope (5:11).

On the other hand, when Christ "is revealed from heaven with His mighty angels in flaming fire," he will render "retribution to those who do not know God and those who do not obey the gospel of our Lord Jesus. And these will pay the penalty of eternal destruction away from the presence of the Lord and from the glory of His power." (II Thess. 1:8,9) Not only will God grant His children relief from their persecutors when He returns again, but He will repay the wicked opponents of the Gospel with affliction (1:6,7).

Paul then exhorts the Thessalonian believers, "stand firm and hold to the traditions which you were taught, whether by word of mouth or by letter from us." (II Thess. 2:15) This is precisely what the evangelicals seek to do by holding to the plain teaching of Scripture concerning these future events- the return of Christ, the resurrection of the body, the final judgment, and the final state of the just and the unjust. What troubles the evangelical is the tendency of many theologians today, including John Mbiti, to flirt with the notion of a universal salvation for all people and a denial of the future hope of the believers as historically understood by the Christian Church.

Until liberal rationalism arose, these biblical truths of eschatology were embraced by the whole Christian Church. The older modernism of Schleiermacher rejected those beliefs as unacceptable to modern man, and Bultmann has reinterpreted these concepts to make them more compatible to this generation. It is a tragedy that Mbiti does not recognize this. Nor does he give any consideration to the evangelical interpretation. Nowhere in his book on eschatology does he give even passing reference to the historic Christian view of eschatology. Mbiti is like the Principal of a theological college in East Africa some years ago who removed all conservative books from the library and placed them in a back room so that students would not have access to them. Mbiti acts as though evangelical eschatology is not worthy of consideration. Indeed, it is dangerous and should not even be studied. It is treated as some extreme doctrine which he calls "exclusively 'futurist'" (Mbiti 1971:51).

Elsewhere, Mbiti complains of the "Theological Impotence" of western theology in Africa (Mbiti 1974a). In a very clever story he writes of a young African theologian who studied overseas and returned to his African peoples. During the great celebration welcoming him back with great pride, a sister became demon possessed. He first recommended the hospital, but that was impossible, for it was 50 miles away.

The chief says to him, 'You have been studying theology overseas for ten years. Now help your sister. She is troubled by the spirit of her great aunt.' He looks around. Slowly he goes to get Bultmann, looks at the index, finds what he wants, reads again about spirit possession in the New Testament. Of course he gets the answer: Bultmann has demythologized it.
(Mbiti 1974:252)

Mbiti concludes by saying, "This theology is largely ignorant of, and often embarrassingly impotent in the face of, human questions in the churches of Africa ... Thus the church has become kerygmatically universal, but is still theologically provincial." (1974a:253)

What Mbiti does not recognize is that the theological impotence is due to liberal theology, not biblical theology. Bultmann's theology is also impotent in the West, as evidenced by the alarming decrease in church membership among those who have "contextualized" their theology to accommodate the modern naturalistic mentality. Every single theologian which this imaginary theological student researched in the West is a liberal. The evangelical theology of the historic Christian Church was apparently never examined. The education of this poor theological student was narrow and provincial.

Mbiti pleads for relevant theology which will address the concerns of the Church in Africa which he enumerates as follows: "National Survival (Liberation, revolution, African culture, racism), Community survival (tribe, clan, age groups, drought, famine, pestilence, calamities), and Personal survival (health, healing, slums, housing, school, fees, clothes, witchcraft, magic, and sorcery)." Now we readily admit that African pastors, teachers and theologians ought to relate Scripture to these contemporary needs. That is vital. To ignore them is to dichotomize life into the earthly and heavenly concerns.

But the distressing fact is that in this article referred to above, Mbiti mentions no need to address the spiritual problems of man which are in fact the root cause for all forms of selfishness. If African Christian Theology merely deals with those issues Mbiti mentions, this theology will also be impotent, for it will deal with the symptom and not the root cause. The fallacy of contemporary theology is the hope that we can humanize cultures by tackling the structures, without dealing with the basic spiritual problem of man. Any social structure will become oppressive without the transformation of the human heart. For God must change the heart of man through the new birth in order for there to be any improvement in relationships. God must be sanctifying His people by His Spirit and through His Word if men are to love one another in a warm hearted community. Mbiti complains that the church is "theologically provincial" but he fails to deal with those theological themes of the Scriptures which are universal. We need to "contextualize" Scripture but we also need to let Scripture "de-contextualize" us. If we only pick and choose those crumbs that suit us, then we do not allow God to communicate "the whole counsel of the Word of God."

In a more recent publication Professor Mbiti does seem to strike a more balanced emphasis. He calls for a holistic view of salvation which includes both the spiritual and physical. He observes that some missionaries "proclaimed a restrictive understanding of salvation from sin and largely for the soul." (1986:156) Mbiti rightly contends that for the Gospel to be meaningful to the African people, "salvation has to embrace their total world, both physical and spiritual." (1986:158) The power of Jesus Christ must be realized in the whole of life, including the domain of sickness and demon possesssion.

But in practice the frequent call for a holistic view of salvation by contemporary theologians turns out to be anything but holistic. Their whole emphasis is on the horizontal with little said of our vertical relationship with God. While stressing the present aspect of the kingdom of God, little explicit teaching is actually given concerning the future realities of the kingdom. Hopefully, Professor Mbiti has begun to modify his theological stance. We look forward to reading his future publications which stress those vital biblical themes characteristic of the historic Christian faith.

**Illustration of Distorted Theology:** "Time" plays an important part both in John Mbiti's analysis of traditional religion and in his theologizing. He has suggested that the African concept of time is "the key to our understanding of the basic religious and philosophical concepts. The concept of time may help to explain beliefs, attitudes, practices and general way of life of African peoples not only in the traditional set up but also in the modern situation." (Mbiti 1969:16)

Not only is time "the key" to Mbiti's understanding of African Traditional Religion, but time is his chief theological concern in his major theological treatise, **New Testament Eschatology in an African Background** (1971). He contends that the African peoples traditionally have not thought much of the distant future. In fact, the African languages (particularly the ones he has analyzed) are incapable of communicating distant future beyond two years. In contrast to this African traditional phenomenon, the pioneering mission among his Akamba people, the Africa Inland Mission, taught an eschatology with the emphasis on the future. Hence, Mbiti contends that the A.I.M. did not faithfully contextualize the Gospel for a people whose language was incapable of expressing distant future.

Since Mbiti constructs his ideas of the African concept of time on the Akamba concept of time and history (Mbiti 1971:24-32), and since his theological views of eschatology relate to this traditional concept of time, it is quite illuminating to consider in some detail this question of time. For it becomes a painful illustration of a distorted theology. Liberal theology is here being introduced into Africa in the guise of African Christian Theology.

## Mbiti's Analysis of Time

Mbiti begins by saying, "For the Akamba, Time is not an academic concern; it is simply a composition of events that have occurred, these which are taking place now and those which will immediately occur." (Mbiti 1971:24)

Time reckoning, therefore, is based on concrete events and not on numerical calendars. Numerical calendars with days, months and years are unknown to Africa. Instead, "phenomenon calendars" (Mbiti 1969:19) are used which dates life on the basis of significant concrete events, such as a particular drought, pestilence, or earthquake. "Dating is done not in relation to an abstract scale, but in relation to particular events which are known to have occurred." (Parratt 1977:119) Time is important at the point of the event and not at the mathematical moment.

A second major point of Mbiti is that "according to traditional concepts, time is a two-dimensional phenomenon, with a long past, a present and virtually no future." (1969:17) "The future as we know it in the linear conception of Time is virtually non-existent in Akamba thinking. My findings from other African peoples have not yielded any radical difference." (1971:24) The future is conceived of primarily as the rhythmic succession of events, the cycle of known and repeated occurrences. Annually, this relates to the planting season, rains and harvest and dry season, which are known and repeated cyclical events. In the life of individuals the future is thought of in terms of birth, marriage, bearing children and death. Thus the future is brief and incorporates what is normal and customary. "The 'sasa' [Kiswahili for 'present'] 'swallows' up what in western or linear concept of time would be considered as the future." (Mbiti 1969:22)

Mbiti claims to base his understanding of the Akamba and other African peoples on the "analyses of myths and language." Most African peoples have myths of the past, myths of creation, the origin of man, the coming of death. "The significant point for our purposes here," Mbiti declares, "is that there are no myths about the future, as far as I have been able to gather from all the available sources that record African myths and stories." (1971:25) Therefore, it would appear "that the future dimension of Time has not been formulated and assimilated into the mythology of African thinking and conception of the universe." (1971:25)

Linguistically, Mbiti has analyzed the tense patterns of eight East African languages, including Kikamba. Of the nine tenses in Kikamba, only three refer to the future, "an extremely limited range of the future stretching to about six months, and in any case not beyond two years from NOW" (1971:27). Mbiti makes some categorical statements about the impossibility of Kikamba expressing distant future.

> People cannot articulate what is in the distant future; they cannot speak about it and cannot, therefore, form myths about it. The Kikamba language is incapable of sustaining such a reality. Only what is in the rhythm of natural phenomena (day and night, rain and dry seasons, birth, marriage and death etc.) can be thought about and expected to take place as it has always been. (1971:27)

Therefore, **zamani,** (Kiswahili for "past"), is the focus of traditional concern. The forefathers who once lived in the present have slipped back into the past. From them the living receive direction and guidance. Those people living now in the present are destined some day to slip into the world of the spirits, slip into **zamani** (past) and continue to give guidance and direction to those in the present.

There is no concept of an eschatological future or golden age. What the people know now will always be. There is no anticipation of the cataclysmic end of the world or some future judgment. What will be is what has always been. Mbiti acknowledges, however, that "a future dimension of Time is being born in Akamba thinking and life. This is partly due to the Christian concept of Eschatology, and partly to a western type education ..." (1971:31)

**Zamani** has its own "past," "present," and "future." Even as a person goes through a process in becoming human, (passing through the various rites of passage in life), even so "death is a process which removes a person gradually from the 'sasa' period to the **'zamani'** " (1969:25) When the living die they enter the recent past when the living-dead are remembered. But gradually they slip further and further into **zamani.** After five generations no one can remember them by name. At that time they lose their "personal immortality" and enjoy a mere "collective immortality" when they are mere "its," unknown by name. When the living-dead cease to "live," they become more greatly feared by the living who no longer know them by name.

Mbiti concludes, that "the traditional concept of time is intimately bound up with the entire life of the people, and our understanding of it may help to pave the way for understanding the thinking, attitude and actions of the people." (1968:28)

## Scholarly Appraisal of Mbiti

Mbiti's interpretation of the African's concept of time, particularly his assertion that the distant future is non-existent and meaningless, has stirred up much criticism and outright repudiation. Some condemn the idea as "nonsense."

Although Mbiti claims to base his conclusions on eight East African languages, including Luganda (Mbiti 1971:26), Kato reports the conversation he had with a Harvard Ph. D. Buganda by the name of Balintuma Kalibala who

> strongly rejected the notion that Africans cannot conceive of the future. When I asked if Buganda of Uganda are among the 'other African societies' who share this supposed Akamba belief, Kalibala replied, 'This is absurd. The African theologian who believes that kind of thing is following what Europeans have taught him. He has not been home to find out things for himself.' He then added, 'we absolutely believe in the future.' (Kato 1975:61)

Another Buganda, Dr. A. Lugira of the Makerere University said, "Professor Mbiti is giving his own opinion; it is academic. His basis is Akamba, and that should be limited there. My people, Buganda, do have a future concept of time." (Kato 1975:62)

Another critic comments,

> While it is correct to observe, as others have, that in Africa 'there is no concept of history moving 'forward' towards a definite future climax', it is

clearly distorting things to represent the African concept of time as the mirror opposite of the Western notion, so that 'history moves backward', from the present, ending up on the past, which is a permanent 'graveyard of time'. This is patently absurd. (Ray 1972a:83)

Other scholars, however, have been more generous toward Mbiti. "Dr. Mbiti has grown up in the culture of which he is writing," comments Newell Booth. "He could be wrong, or he could have expressed his views poorly but it is unlikely that what he says is 'patently absurd'." (Booth 1975:82)

John Parratt gives a thoughtful assessment of the whole issue. In evaluating Mbiti's thesis of time, Parratt says that if Mbiti has correctly interpreted the data, "he may well be justified in his claim to have found the key to the understanding of African religious philosophy." (Parratt 1977:118)

It may be said at once, that the idea of the future only becomes meaningful on a linear view of time - time conceived in terms of a straight line, progressing from one point to the next towards an ultimate end. This view of time is not found in Eastern religions, is absent from ancient Greek science and represents a fairly late development even in European thought. It is furthermore not characteristic of primitive thought generally. It would be surprising therefore if it were found to be typical of African thought. (Parratt 1977:118)

Parratt himself rejects the notion that Africans embrace a linear view of time. He believes that "the most common way of regarding time in traditional societies is in calendrical terms." (Parratt 1977:119) By this he means that time is reckoned by the seasonal rituals and concrete events. Cyclical view of time has "deep roots" in the history of mankind, being represented by ancient Greece. For them time was rooted in the past and the Greeks were therefore "backward-looking."

To this extent Parratt agrees with Mbiti. "However, to acknowledge the importance of the past does not necessarily commit us to diminishing the importance of the present or to abolishing the future from African thought." (1977:121) Parratt continues,

The question of the future time is more complex. The linguistic evidence remains to be competently assessed, but the indications are that the case may not all be on Mbiti's side. Further, that African societies did have some conceptions of passage of the time is surely evident in that the rites of passages through which the individuals had to pass - birth, initiation, marriage, death - cannot be conceived in any other way than as a progression. From the standpoint of the individual there must have been some conception of an advance of time. While this may not strictly be linear time, it does involve the idea of development through various set stages which have a temporal reference. A mere forward-looking attitude cannot therefore have been completely absent from traditional thought. (Parratt (1977:122)

In a very carefully balanced paper Parratt asserts that the linear concept of time is traced by biblical scholarship to "the Judaeo-Christian tradition."

Cullmann points out that the Christian teaching tended to be "eschatological," moving to a **telos.**

The linear concept of time proves to be as much an alien imposition upon African thought as it was upon the ancient world. In traditional Africa time is neither conceived of in a linear fashion, nor does it move towards an eschatological telos. In so far as the linear method of time reckoning is employed it represents a foreign element, which may be regarded as part of the legacy of Western Christianity or of colonial influence. (Parratt 1977:123)

In conclusion Parratt concurs with Mbiti that the traditional African concept of time was not linear and that African societies "are predominatly backward-looking."

On balance therefore it appears that a good deal of evidence may be brought in support of Professor Mbiti's thesis. While he has perhaps been inclined to overstate his case, his claim that in traditional African thought there is 'virtually no future' commands a good deal of evidence, and to say that African societies are more orientated towards the past than towards the future is to reflect a view which has been frequently voiced by social anthropologists. (Parratt 1977:123)

## Critical Appraisal of Mbiti

Through field research we conclude that many of Mbiti's concepts are valid (See end note). Time is indeed reckoned by concrete events. A Mukamba will say, "I was born before the great famine." "I will come to your house before the sun gets hot." Women waited until the cock crowed the first time to know how long it would be until dawn. Men used the position of the moon to know when they should go to the fields and kill the animals which destroyed their crops at night. Before the advent of the calendar and watch there was no other way of reckoning time.

Time was not considered in the abstract. Until the events took place, no one could know exactly what would occur. One Mukamba compared time to a ball of cotton thread. Not until the string is unraveled can people know whether there are knots or what the thickness of the string is. Though people can see the ball of string, it does not become vivid until the ball is unraveled.

However, Mbiti has in fact been "inclined to overstate the case," when he writes, "the people cannot articulate what is in the distant future." This judgment is based on the persistent and vigorous reaction of the Akamba themselves when discussing this topic over the past nine years.

How can the Akamba today embrace the concept of an eschatological future if "the Kikamba language is incapable of sustaining" the reality of a distant future, as Mbiti maintains? The eschatological teaching of the Africa Inland Mission, begun in Ukambani in 1895, is described by Mbiti. The A.I.M. taught the historic Christian view of the second coming of Christ and all the events that surround this eschatological hope. He calls this an "exclusively 'futuristic' eschatology." Mbiti complains that "The teaching of the Africa Inland Mission in Ukambani has stressed almost exclusively a few aspects of the 'futuristic' element of Eschatology, thereby, a) coming into serious conflict with the linguistic and conceptual understanding of the Akamba." (1971:57) Any cross cultural communication of the Gospel must consider the "deeper level of Akamba conceptual understanding" before Christian teaching is possible (1971:58). Mbiti concludes that difficulties in comprehension where inevitable. Yet Mbiti readily admits, "This missionary teaching has had a tremendous impact upon Akamba Christians." (1971:56) The fact is that the Akamba A.I.C. Christians fully embrace the eschatological hope of the evangelical churches and do not exhibit any problems with comprehension. How can this be, if "the Kikamba language is incapable of sustaining" the concept of a distant future?

**Mbiti bases his conclusion on** two kinds of evidence: traditional myths and **linguistic structure. The** Akamba agree that there are no traditional myths of the **future. The Akamba** traditionally have lived more for the present and thought **less of the future. The** future was not stressed. There is not a single word in **Kikamba traditionally** used for the "future." The future was guided by the past **traditions. But the fact** is that the traditional Akamba were capable of speaking of **the future and in fact did so.**

On pages 26 and 27 in his book, **New Testament Eschatology in an African Background,** Mbiti records nine verb tenses in Kikamba. While the Akamba informants agreed with Mbiti's analysis of the past tenses, they believe he distorts the future tenses. The far and indefinite past in Kikamba may be indicated by doubling the vowel. The eighth and ninth verb tenses listed by Mbiti and referring to the unspecified or remote past are made by the doubling of the vowels, "oo". His interpretation of the approximate time for the eighth tense, is "any day before yesterday," and for the ninth tense, "no specific time in the distant past." In other words, the context determines whether it is recent or more remote in the past.

The future is indicated in the same manner many times, by doubling the vowel, though there is no uniformity in this throughout Ukambani. **Ningooka** means "I will come," **ngatwaana** means "I will marry," and **ngaakw'a**, means "I will die." In John 14:3 the verb used to translate the indefinite future of Christ's second coming is **ngooka,** "I will come again." Once again it is the context which determines how distant the future is. Mbiti arbitrarily states that the approximate time period is "about two to six months from now" or "within a foreseeable while, after such and such an event."

The fact is that no Kikamba grammar affirms what Mbiti here affirms. The indefinite future tense is formed the same way as the indefinite past. Usage of the language by the people determines the meaning. The Akamba in fact do manifest by the usage of their language that they do conceive of the distant future. Those Akamba in my acquaintance categorically assert that it is absurd to say that the Kikamba language is incapable of conveying a distant future.

The story is told of Nzau who had a quarrel with his father and in the struggle the son hurt his father on the forehead. Nzau lived for many years, marrying and bearing children. His friends and neighbors all believed that some day Nzau would be beaten by his own children. In fact this happened. Nzau in a private conversation acknowledged that he knew from the time that he fought with his father, that some day his own son would beat him. And this was in the distant future, more than two years as arbitrarily specified by Mbiti.

Blessings also involved several generations to come. An old man would bless a young person, saying, "May God bless you and keep you to grow to reach where

I have reached," or "May God keep you so that you will live to see your grandchildren."

There was a conflict between a husband and wife in Ukambani and the two were about to separate. They vowed to stay separate until their bodies were put into the grave. They went so far as to say, "My bones and your bones will never agree to lie together even when put into the same grave."

The story is told of Thitu and his friend who migrated to the land of the Gikuyu during drought time. While there they were badly treated. They vowed that when God blessed them with children, they would educate their sons so that they would not suffer the same problems they suffered due to lack of education. This is an example of future orientation and future planning, for neither of them were married at that time.

When the Akamba near Mwingi, Kitui, built a stone house for some white people, the Akamba commented, "This house will be here longer than our children and grandchildren." These people were looking 100 years into the future.

The life of a stone house is much longer than the traditional Akamba is accustomed to, it is true. Very little in the Akamba traditional material culture has potential for permanency. The hides traditionally used for beds may last seven years, if the termites do not first devour them. The grass roof might hold up for 20 years, but that is unusual. Though the traditional Akamba does not devote much of his time thinking of the distant future, he is very capable of doing this and in fact does.

Two young Akamba were great friends. In fact so close were they in their comradeship that they decided to perpetuate their friendship even after their death by vowing that the daughter of one would marry the son of the other man. This was many years prior to the event, for they were not even married yet. When they were finally married, one man had a daughter and the other a son. When those offspring reached the age for marriage, their fathers made known to them their previous vows. This whole process involved many years of planning and waiting.

One Mukamba recommended that a missionary marry several wives so that he could form his own clan. The missionary already had nine children and the thought was that with many wives he could become a great man, in traditional terms. Such thinking involves several generations, planning for the distant future.

However, one could argue that all these examples are anticipated experiences within the normal life cycle. They are not categorically new or unknown. But this is the normal way of thinking among human beings. Even in the Scriptures, the revelation of the apocalyptic end times is in terms of the known experiences of people who lived then.

One source of evidence omitted by Mbiti is the existence of traditional prophets. Akamba prophets were famous for their ability to predict unusual and distant events. Syokimau, for instance, prophesied that the white men would come, that there would be a snake stretching from Mombasa to Lake Victoria, and that people would carry fire in their pockets. The snake turned out to be the

Uganda railroad and the fire in the pockets referred to the matches. Prophets such as Syokimau did predict unusual events in the indefinite future.

While the Akamba vigorously reject Mbiti's concept that the Kikamba language is incapable of conceiving of the distant future, that a future beyond two years was not known traditionally, we do accept his contention that the past is stressed more than the future. People look to the past to draw lessons for the present. Present prosperity depends on the right relationship with the past. One's relations with the ancestors determines the success or failure in the present. Children are taught stories of the past to teach them morality. The past has an unlimited store of events from which the people can draw lessons. Events of the past are burned into the memory of the people as their history is retold and learned. The past is the foundation of the future.

But Mbiti stresses a long past. In fact, the memories of time beyond a few years become very vague. Traditionally, generations are remembered up to the fifth or sixth generation. Beyond this time, ancestors are not remembered. Thus the distant past is blurred. The same of course is true of the future which is only vaguely perceived. Kenyatta speaks of "the dim past" being recalled by the stories told among the Gikuyu (1966:1).

As Mbiti declares, it appears that events are moving into the past. While time moves forward, the events seem to move backward. One might illustrate this by a moving bus with people inside. While the bus is actually moving forward, the objects outside the bus appear as though they were moving backward. The Akamba do traditionally think of and plan for the future. But their orientation is more toward the past. In this context time does appear to move backward.

In these days Christianity has loosened the potential of the Akamba in their future orientation. Through Christ the fear of the spirits is being removed. Therefore, people are more free to speak of the future. Failure to speak of the future and plan for it in traditional Akamba culture, may be closely tied to the traditional fear of spirits. The Gospel has not merely taught them to be future oriented through the teaching of the second coming of Christ. The message of Christ has liberated them so that they can think more freely of the future without traditional fears of witchcraft, ancestors and other mystical powers.

In traditional Akamba society the people are ruled by the elders. The most highly esteemed elders are those who have slipped into **zamani,** first becoming the living-dead and after five generations becoming mere spirits without personal identification. These **aimu** who have now entered the past are the guardians of the Akamba traditions. The evil persons in society today, the **aoi,** seek to disrupt society through the powers within the universe. The diviners, the **andu awe,** seek to counteract the evil power through recourse to greater powers they find from the **aimu,** also from the past. The present customs and practices are traditions handed down from the past. The **aimu** resist any change from the past traditions. The Akamba do not envision any future changes. There will be no future utopia or restoration of good. What is present is good. The present is what has always been and what will always be. Thus the traditional Akamba are more "backward looking" than future oriented. This has resulted in the maintenance of the status quo in the past.

But the Christian Gospel has liberated the Akamba so that they can exercise their potential in dealing with the future creatively.

This fact that the Gospel has provided a new concept of time, moving forward toward a goal, instead of looking backward to traditions, has occurred repeatedly throughout history. Cullmann notes that the New Testament concept of time is the opposite to that of the Greeks.

> We must start from this fundamental perception, that the symbol of time for Primitive Christianity as well as for Biblical Judaism and the Iranian religion is the LINE, while in Hellenism it is the CIRCLE. Because in Greek thought time is not conceived as a progressing line with beginning and end, but rather a circle, the fact that man is bound to time must here be experienced as an enslavement, as a curse. Time moves about in the eternal circular course in which everything keeps recurring. (Cullmann 1964:50)

Traditional Africans were very much like traditional Greeks before the coming of the Gospel in being cyclically oriented and backward looking. Christianity has given a new perspective on time. Even secular western culture which has disowned its Christian origins has retained the linear concept of time.

It is also true that the encroachment of western civilization which includes schools and urbanization has brought with it liberation. For instance, in rural areas the Luo do not talk much about what they will do in the future. Nor do they invest resources in the education of their children for fear of witchcraft. Many Luo move into the urban areas in order to escape the fears of witchcraft, spirits and ancestors. When the Luo desire to invest in the future, they move to an urban area such as Nairobi. When the Luo moves to the urban area he then begins planning for and investing in the future. This is not due to the fact that westernization has invented the future concept for him. But the removal from his home area with strong traditions has liberated him to be free in planning for the future.

Thus we find that the traditional Akamba concept of time is fast eroding. As Christians set an example of planning for the future, as schools and government encourage plans for development, so the older traditions are breaking down. Yet they persist. Much of the behaviour of the Akamba today cannot be properly understood without a knowledge of this basic element in their traditional world view, the traditional belief in time.

We conclude this critical appraisal of John Mbiti by observing that he has made two fundamental errors: first is his assessment of the traditional concept of time and the second is his theological understanding of the Scriptures. He has criticized mission Christianity among his people because he alleges they did not contextualize the Gospel to suit the mentality of the Akamba. The A.I.M. was in error, Mbiti states, for stressing the futuristic aspects of eschatology - the second coming of Christ as historically taught by the Christian Church. Eschatological teaching concerning the second advent should have been more oriented to the

70

present, Mbiti contends, for in fact the Akamba were incapable of conceiving any future beyond two years.

This twin error of Mbiti's - an ethnological and theological error - has been eulogized by some as a refreshing example of contextualizing by Africans today. However, a careful study has revealed that Mbiti's understanding of biblical eschatology and his perception of African belief in time have been distorted. How tragic! If the African Christian Church is to remain evangelical in her convictions, there must be greater faithfulness to the Word of God. We must allow Scripture to "de-contextualize" us so that we can be liberated to be what God has created us to be. And we ought not distort African traditions to suit our liberalizing tendencies.

## Byang Kato

Among all the African theologians who have written thus far, the late Byang Kato is the one who has addressed these questions of theological pitfalls in Africa the most forthrightly. On the one hand, Kato taught the need for respect of the African traditional heritage. He believed that evangelicals should contextualize the Gospel. On the other hand, he warned evangelicals of liberal theology being introduced under the cloak of African Christian Theology.

Kato recognized the inadequacy of former judgments made of African Traditional Religion (1975: 18-24). He also accepted the need for cultural authenticity, for he says, "The search for authenticity through culture remains a desirable element in many African societies. The attitude of Christians toward cultural renaissance need not be negative." (1976:146)

Kato also recognized the need for more relevant theology in Africa. Kato spoke, saying, "This writer senses the need for Christian theology to address itself specifically to the African situation. Areas such as principles of interpretation, polygamy, family life, the spirit world and communal life should be given serious consideration." (Kato 1976:146) For this reason he does not suggest "a moratorium on further research on African thought patterns." (Kato:147)

But Byang Kato was greatly exercised by the fact that he perceived African Theology turning more to African Traditional Religion as a source of theology, than to the Scriptures. Kato lamented, "Theology in Africa is increasingly turning to African traditional religions rather than to the Bible as its absolute source." (Kato 1976:147) He regretted that many theologians were spending most of their time defending African Traditional Religions and practices which are "incompatible with biblical teaching." (1976:146) "In the African evangelicals' effort to express Christianity in the context of the African, the Bible must remain the absolute source. The Bible is God's written Word addressed to Africans - and to all peoples - within their cultural background." (1976:148)

It is significant that Kato made a statement which is almost a carbon copy of the statement made by Mbiti. "The noble desire to indigenize Christianity in Africa must not be forsaken. An indigenous theology is a necessity. But one must not betray Scriptural principles of God and His dealing with man at the altar of any regional theology." (Kato 1975:16) Kato, like Mbiti, recognized the need to

71

develop a more relevant theology for Africa. Kato, like Mbiti, stressed the need to make the Bible our primary source.

Why then do they differ in their outcome? Kato makes many critical assessments of John Mbiti and Bolaji Idowu, devoting three chapters to Mbiti and two chapters to Idowu, a total of 70 pages out of a total of 184 in the book. Mbiti speaks of Kato launching "a most bitter attack on myself, Professor E.B. Idowu and ecumenism." (Appiah-Kubi 1979:85) If both are concerned about the two poles inherent in African Christian Theology, the Bible as the primary source and the context of African religion and culture, why should they clash in such a fundamental way? Did Kato simply misunderstand Mbiti, as Professor Mbiti claims? (1986:48)

We readily admit that the late Byang Kato was a fledgeling young theologian who made some errors when interpreting several of the African theologians (cf. Bowers 1980). However, his fundamental concern for the spread of syncretistic liberal theology in Africa, and in particular, the creeping universalism within some theological circles, is correct. His warning of the liberal pitfalls in African Christian Theology is most relevant for evangelicals even today.

But the question remains. If Kato like Mbiti was concerned about the primacy of Scripture in all theologizing, and if Kato like Mbiti was concerned about an authentic and relevant theology in Africa which utilized African thought patterns, then why did Kato clash with Mbiti in such a forthright manner?

The answer is quite plain. Byang Kato approached the Scriptures with full confidence in its unity and authority because the Holy Spirit is the Divine Author. Believing in the plenary, verbal inspiration of Scripture, Kato did not doubt the full authority of Scripture. There are no conflicting, variant traditions in the Bible from which one can pick and choose as he pleases. The Bible is not merely a witness or testimony of the first Christian community. Nor is it the means of revelation. Kato interpreted Scripture as the inerrant Word of God, using the grammatico-historical hermeneutical principles which are fundamental for all evangelical hermeneutics. This does not guarantee total agreement as can be amply demonstrated. But despite the many differences among evangelicals, there is marked unity on all the "fundamentals" of the faith. And this is due to the fact that evangelicals take seriously the plain teaching of Scripture.

Kato affirms,

> ...the search for an African personality should not lead Africans to a compromising position. This is not to suggest a moratorium on further research on African thought patterns. But in the African evangelical effort to express Christianity in the context of Africa, the Bible must remain the absolute source. The Bible is God's written Word addressed to Africans - and to all peoples - within their cultural background. (1985:43)

In contrast, Mbiti approaches Scripture as "a human advisor" (Appiah-Kubi 1979:91). We ask, in what sense is the Bible only our human advisor? In what sense does the Holy Spirit advise us apart from and contrary to the plain teaching of Scripture? True, the 66 books of the Bible were written by prophets and apostles in such a way that their personalities were fully utilized. In no sense was Scripture dictated by the Holy Spirit. Writing styles of the various human authors all reflect their personalities, educational background, personal experiences and unique historical situations.

Nevertheless, the Scripture affirms that these human authors were superintended by the Holy Spirit in such a way that everything they taught is true. These human instruments "were moved by the Holy Spirit," "they spoke from God," "no prophecy was ever made by an act of human will." (II Pet. 1:21) Evangelicals believe that the Bible is God's Word, fully inspired in every part, extending to the choice of words in the original manuscripts. We affirm that the Bible is fully human and fully divine and without error in anything that it teaches. The nature of the Bible is thus to some extent analogous to the incarnation, in that Jesus Christ is truly human and truly divine, yet being without sin. The Bible is truly human and truly divine in its origins and yet without error in all that it teaches.

Regrettably, the Scriptures are torn apart by Mbiti through critical scholarship. For instance Mbiti claims, "There is no single or consistent view of Time in the Bible. Instead we find several views of Time." (Mbiti 1971:38) He claims that the western concept of linear time has been imposed on the Scriptures and thereby has caused "much harm" to Christian thinking which has placed too much emphasis on the futuristic aspect of eschatology.

Through his selective use of Scripture, he promotes universalism, hoping and believing all peoples will be saved, to enjoy a heaven which is primarily "theocentric worship and fellowship" and which "defies description in terms of Space and Time." (Mbiti 1971:86,179) Having spiritualized the various eschatological imageries of Scripture throughout his book and having developed a modified form of realized eschatology, without really committing himself to future realities of the second coming of Christ, Mbiti concludes:

> There is not a single soul, however debased or even unrepentant, which can successfully 'flee' from the Spirit of God...the harmony of the heavenly worship would be impaired if, out of the one hundred in the sheepfold, there is one soul, which continues to languish in Sheol or the 'lake of fire'. (1971:179)

Kato was biblical and historically correct to be concerned with the spread of implicit and explicit universalism on the continent of Africa. In addition to universalism being in theological vogue throughout the west, we have additional factors here in Africa. "An emotional touch," as Kato said, "out of genuine love for the ancestors who die without the knowledge of the way of salvation, is a big attraction to universalism." (Kato 1975:13)

For us to pretend that there is no problem is to become blind to the facts. Loss of biblical authority in ecumenical circles has led to a departure from the historic Christian faith. Tokumboh Adeyemo, the General Secretary of the Association of Evangelicals of Africa and Madagascar, laments,

> Concentrated efforts are being made in our universities and other places of higher learning to produce theology for our churches, but the out-

put so far cannot be truly called 'Christian.' The proponents of this African theology, however, not only use Christian terminology, but claim to be Christians ... In the African evangelicals' effort to express Christianity in the context of the African, the Bible must remain the absolute source. (Adeyemo 1979b:16)

It seems regrettable that we must engage in polemics. How much better would it be if we could all live and let live. Division in the Christian Church is lamentable. Would that we could agree with Mbiti when he pleads, "There is enough room for each one of us to make a scholarly contribution without resorting to groundless attacks on others, even if one may hold different opinions or interpretations of the Scriptures." (1986:49) Within the fold of orthodoxy there ought to be room for different opinions without groundless attacks on others.

Yet liberal Christianity is another religion, not the historic Christian faith. When the foundation of Christian authority is emaciated through a low view of Scripture, when the fundamental elements of the Gospel are altered by accomodation to rationalism, we are compelled to speak out in fidelity to Jesus Christ our Lord and Saviour. Evangelicals seek to follow the admonition of Jude, the servant and brother of Jesus Christ who appealed to his readers, "that you contend earnestly for the faith which was once for all delivered to the saints." (Jude 1:3) And this is what the late Byang Kato has tried to do together with countless other evangelicals throughout the continent.

Though Byang Kato has been criticized as being unduly negative in his book, the fact is that he concluded it with a "Ten Point Proposal" for evangelicals to follow in safeguarding biblical Christianity in Africa. One of those points was to "concentrate effort on the training of men in the Scriptures, employing the original languages to facilitate their ability in exegeting the Word of God in depth." (1975:182)

Through the personal promotion of Kato as the first African General Secretary of the Association of Evangelicals of Africa and Madagascar (AEAM), two graduate schools of theology have been established, one in francophone speaking Africa (Bangui Evangelical School of Theology in the Central African Republic) and a second one in anglophone Africa (the Nairobi Evangelical Graduate School of Theology in Kenya).

It is significant that within the By-Laws of the Graduate School in Kenya one objective has been stated as follows:

To provide courses which in every case, to whatever degree is practicable and necessary, will be oriented to Africa and its circumstances, problems and needs. To present the unchanging Christian faith to students through the perspective of African culture and world-view. To develop a sufficient awareness among church leaders of the relevant philosophies, ideologies, and problems that will enable them to contextualize the Gospel and apply it to the life situation of their people. To incarnate the eternal and unchanging truth of God in the lives of the people in Africa thus making it meaningful and readily applicable to every need. To relate all taught theology to the contemporary and local culture and African thought processes. To present biblical truth in its relation to African questions and problems and those that are relevant to Africa. To ensure that every aspect of the training given shall contribute to these goals, without making the course parochial or neglecting world-wide theological problems and the world-wide commission of the church. (NEGST By-Laws p. 1)

Though the objective as stated above was not composed by the late Byang Kato himself, he would have heartily supported this goal for the Evangelical Graduate School. Indeed, the whole task of proclaiming "the unchanging Christian faith" to the peoples "through the perspective of African culture and world-view" was the burden of Kato and all those evangelicals who share his evangelical convictions. Kato together with all evangelicals on the African continent are seeking to establish an African Christian faith which will be, in Kato's words, "truly biblical and truly African."

This is evidenced by the A.E.A.M. sponsored Theological Education by Extension programme (TEE) and the Christian Learning Materials Centre (CLMC). CLMC is preparing Sunday School materials for all ages, written by Africans and for Africans. It is tested in the field to ascertain its relevance and effectiveness. TEE provides a full Bible School course of materials for the training of lay church leaders, written for African believers in the African context and to be studied by them in extension.

As we all know, the task of implementing our ideas is not easy. Evangelicals have no private access to the royal road of contextualizing the Gospel. Their dreams are more dramatic than their actual implementation. But the fact is that evangelicals like Byang Kato and the members of the Association of Evangelicals of Africa and Madagascar and others of like mind are busily engaged in the task of making the Gospel incarnate in African culture.

# GUIDELINES FOR DEVELOPING AFRICAN CHRISTIAN THEOLOGY

Anyone who has observed both the erection of a large building and the demolition of another will recall the striking contrast. Only with great care and much time can a large building be erected. However, its destruction takes place in short order and with a loud crash.

We have taken some time in the painful examination of attempts by good people to construct an African Christian Theology. We have sought to disclose the faulty foundation upon which they have begun the task. With a low view of Scripture no theology will stand the test of time. Like so much of the experimental theologies of the West these days, they will last a few short years and then be bypassed for newer, "more relevant theology."

In the first section of this chapter we have sought to point out the unbiblical presuppositions which help shape much of the methodology for African Christian Theology. In this sense our purpose has been negative.

The major question for evangelicals is this, "How shall we develop African Christian Theology?" Having traced the historical development, we are conscious that the foundational task for all theological reflection is the development of methodology that is both consistent with Scripture and workable in our African context. A faulty methodology will lead to a faulty theology even as a poor foundation results in a poorly constructed building.

In this second section our purpose is positive, to propose Guidelines for the development of an evangelical theology in Africa. To build an evangelical theology is more difficult than the demolition of liberal theology. But as evangelicals we must not be content with critical judgments. We must eagerly and energetically construct an evangelical theology for our African context.

We have seen that for African Christian Theology to have any meaning, it must be done mainly by African Christians who are basically African oriented. Given the past history of Africa, any other thought would be dubious. Many Africans today have grown up in Christian homes, removed from traditional religion. After spending years overseas in their studies they have become more bi-cultural than authentically African in their orientation. Authentic African theology can be done by them only with difficulty. Evangelical Africans who are in basic touch with their African context are the main ones who can build an evangelical theology in the African context.

Yet we all learn from one another. And as Kanyandago has said, "Being African is not a necessary condition for doing African Theology otherwise we risk to define it in terms of race and colour." (Kanyandago 1978:342; cf. Dickson 1974:204)

The Third World Theologians affirmed in the Seoul Declaration,

We give thanks to our sovereign God who has preserved and renewed the church during the past nineteen centuries. We express our indebtedness to the creeds of the Early Church, the confessions of the European Reformation, and the spiritual awakening of the revival movements in modern· times. We recognize the contributions western churches and missionary agencies in the birth and growth in many parts of the Third World. (Seoul Declaration 1983:8)

It is within this context of mutuality that we propose the following Guidelines in the attempt to develop an evangelical theology in the African context.

African Christian Theology is in actual fact "contextualized theology." Much has been said and written about the need to have the living Word of God incarnated in the lives and cultures of all people. As evangelical African Christians "respond meaningfully to the Gospel within the framework of their situation," they will be developing evangelical theology in the African context. This is nothing less than contextualized theology. How do we contextualize theology?

Reference has been made in various articles and books to the importance of guidelines but nothing much has been detailed. Imasogie has written a book of 92 pages entitled, **Guidelines for Christian Theology in Africa.** (1983) But regrettably he has devoted only six pages in the book to actual "Proposed Guidelines." And these pages say nothing of methodology. They simply recommend three motifs for Christian theology in Africa.

For an evangelical, the development of guidelines for methodology is most crucial. How do we develop theology in any context? What troubles evangelicals is not that African Christians are reflecting on God's Word, but that some have an unorthodox view of Scripture and that they interpret the Bible in such a manner as not to do justice to the original message of the Bible. As Dickson affirmed in 1974, "African Theology could proceed on the basis of a faulty methodology." (Dickson 1974)

Following is a proposed definition of the process of contextualizing Christian theology together with an expansion of each concept. This is an attempt toward developing a methodology of contextualizing that will make theology both relevant to the context and faithful to the Scriptures.

Contextualizing theology is that 8) dynamic process whereby 1) the people of God 6) living in community and interacting with believers throughout time and space, 4) under the illuminating guidance of the Holy Spirit, 9) proclaim 7) in their own language and thought forms, 5) the Word that God has spoken to them 3) in their context 2) through the study of the Scriptures.

## 1) Contextualizing is Done by the People of God.

Unregenerate men cannot do theology. Nor can individual believers in isolation from the believing community do theology. The study of Scripture and the understanding of the will of God can only be done properly by those who have entered a covenant relationship with the living God through personal faith in Jesus Christ.

Bruce Nicholls speaks of "starting from within the circle of faith-commitment." (Nicholls 1979a:55) Nominal Christians cannot make effective and faithful theologians for the Word of God must be grasped by faith and not merely by the intellect. Christian theologizing is far more than an academic exercise. Without genuinely saving faith we can neither believe that God is nor understand the spiritual insights in the Bible.

We live in a day when professing Christians do not see any relevance in prayer, worship and evangelism as it has been understood historically by the Christian Church. Bishop John Robinson in his book, **Honest to God,** confessed that he and many other seminarians did not see any relevance in the churchly discipline of prayer. James Cone, a Protestant clergyman, rejects the value of prayer during this time of black revolution (Cone 1970:234). The problem with many theologians is that they either do not have a living faith in Jesus Christ, or they do not approach life from within "the circle of faith-commitment."

The contextualizing of biblical theology in a changing world demands a rethinking of the whole process of doing theology. But the Bible itself insists that the starting point must be from within the circle of faith-commitment to God's self-revelation in Christ. With the weakening of assurance of the knowledge of the content of the Christian faith, many theologians and communicators are, in practice, making the cultural context the starting point (Nicholls 1979a:55).

When we speak of the "People of God," we do not mean the elite who know the original languages of the Bible and who have graduate degrees in theology and philosophy. The "people of God" are not restricted to the professors of theology in the universities and theological colleges. The people of God are doing theology at every imaginable level: Christians reading their Bible and applying God's truth to their own lives; lay persons who study Scripture in preparation for teaching, witnessing and preaching; evangelists who study Scripture in order to proclaim the Gospel and bring men and women to faith in Christ; pastors, both ordained and non-ordained, official clergy and lay clergy, who study the Bible in order to preach the Word of God relevantly to the people on Sundays; men with a prophetic ministry who study Scripture in order to call society back to the ways of the living God, ways of justice, and righteousness; teachers who study Scripture in order to instruct students preparing for some greater Christian ministry; scholars who study Scripture in order to write books and articles both at the popular and professional level. The People of God at every level are doing and ought to do theological reflection.

Theological errors causing the most damage to the Christian church usually come from the top and filter down. What is needed in developing African Christian Theology is to involve all Christians in the task of studying the Scriptures. When we listen to the biblical insights of lay people, we are listening to genuinely contextualized theology. Hassing calls this **"theologia in loco,** theology at the grass roots." "Only as the grass roots get involved will Christian answers to African questions be forthcoming." (Hassing 1971:514) Therefore, the actual research involved in developing African Christian Theology must embrace the grass roots level - not to detemine our beliefs by what the majority of people think, like a Gallop Poll, but to gain genuine insight into what the genuine needs and solutions are in the African context according to the Scriptures.

## 2.  Contextualization is Through the Study of Scripture.

If the starting point of the people of God is in "the circle of faith-commitment," the focal point is the study of Scripture which has priority over everything else.

Theologians who outline the various sources of theology, always acknowledge that the Scripture forms a primary source. But in practice the Bible is not normative. For this reason it seems best for evangelicals to acknowledge only one source of theology, namely, the written Word of God. This must be understood through the illumination of the Holy Spirit and in the context of the reader. But the one source of theology can never be confused with or in some way comparable to the context. Scripture, therefore, becomes the One Source for evangelical theology and that one source is normative.

The problem we are dealing with is the relationship between the Bible and context. Karl Barth waged a vigorous war against the old modernists whose "natural theology" ate up "grace" as revealed in Scripture. There is real danger that our cultural heritage will effectively cancel out what God clearly teaches in the Bible. This has been a problem in the past and will continue to be so.

The problem throughout history is that men with good intentions seek to accommodate the Christian faith so as to make it more relevant and acceptable. Today western theologians such as Bultmann, Tillich, John T. Robinson and others seek to make Christianity acceptable to secular man. But in their adjustments to western culture, they have surrendered the heart of the Christian faith. As Donald McGavran has written, these adjustments must be rejected "on the grounds that instead of revelation judging culture, in such adjustments the culture has weighed revelation, found it wanting and folded it into a syncretistic form agreeable to modern man." (Yamaori 1975:45)

The tragedy is that the rationalism of the West has now seeped into the African Church through western scholarship. The western rationalists have provided the "theological" rationale to accommodate the Word of God to the African culture. With the loss of divine authority in Scripture, we are left with no sure standard of truth.

Tutu quotes with approval Maurice Wiles, a western theologian, who said, "There are no fixed criteria for the determination of theological truth and error. We ought therefore to be ready to tolerate a considerable measure even of what seems to us to be error, for we can not be certain that it is we who are right." (Tutu 1975:31) When the Scriptures become a mere witness to the testimony of the people of God, when the words of the Bible no longer are the very Word of God, then man is left to his own subjective opinion as to what is right and wrong.

Fortunately, there is a growing number of African theologians writing and speaking to the issue of the day from the evangelical perspective. Tokumboh Adeyemo calls on evangelical Africans to make a total, unconditional and exclusive commitment to the authority of the Bible. He believes that the theological battle in Africa will be won or lost in the areas of the truths concerning inspiration, infallibility, inerrancy and absolute authority of Scripture (Adeyemo 1979b:16,17). The future vitality of the Christian Church in Africa depends on such commitment by evangelical theologians. Adeyemo has written forthrightly as an evangelical on the question, **Salvation in African Tradition** (1979a).

Having resolved by faith that the Bible is indeed the infallible Word of God, we are then faced with the problem of interpretation. Hermeneutics involves both the subjective and objective elements. The objective element involves the "scientific" approach of the grammatico-historical method of exegesis in which we seek to know the meaning of the text as the original author intended. The subjective element involves the existential involvement of the student in the understanding and appropriation of the text to one's life. This is frequently called the "hermeneutical circle" (Padilla 1979). Nicholls speaks of it as "the objective-subjec-

79

tive principle of distancing from and indentification with the text" (Nicholls 1979a:49).

There is in this a two-way process of encounter. Nicholls seeks to maintain a "balance between the objective authority of the Word of God and the subjective experience of the interpretation."·On the one hand we need to distance ourselves from the text by critical study of the Bible. "The task of exegesis is the recovery of the **sensus literalis,** the literal or natural meaning of the text, involving the right use of the linguistic tools and historical method, traditionally known as the 'grammatico-historical' method." (Nicholls 1978:49) This he distinguishes from the more speculative historical critical method which operates on the documentary hypothesis of Scripture. Instead of us refashioning Scripture, we need to allow the Scripture to refashion our own pre-understanding, "recognizing its objective authority and its internal harmony" (Nicholls 1979a:49).

On the other hand we need to identify with the text. This is "the fusion of the horizons" as the Holy Spirit illumines our hearts. Whereas the neo orthodox accuse the evangelicals of stressing the cold, factual, propositional doctrines of the Bible, we recognize the error of their judgment.

As an evangelical growing up in a Mennonite family, I have always been taught the importance of a spiritual encounter with God Himself when reading the Scriptures. All those in the pietistic tradition of the Christian Faith are familiar with this truth. We believe the essential teachings of the Bible are clearly taught, a principle commonly spoken of as the principle of perspicuity. As believers meditate upon Scripture, the Holy Spirit illuminates the heart. As we approach God in the Scriptures through prayer, He speaks to us regarding our responsibilities in our context. This is the subjective aspect of the hermeneutical principle.

## 3.  The Context of the People of God.

By "context" we refer to the whole environment in which the people of God live, including the social, economic, educational, religious, philosophical and political; in brief, man's culture. Culture is not static and therefore, God must address each generation in each culture through His Word.

Students of the Bible have long since recognized the importance of understanding the biblical context if we are to understand the meaning of the Bible. "The text taken out of context is a pretext," is a truism often repeated.

The emphasis in contextualized theology, however, is that we must also take the context of the present day student of the Bible more seriously. We know that God speaks to us in terms of our concrete, living situations. If we do not understand the Bible as it applies to our own context, we have not truly understood the Bible for ourselves. Thus there is an interplay between the Bible and our context.

"The Willowbank Report" on Gospel and Culture, sponsored by the Lausanne Comittee for World Evangelization, explains the contextual approach.

It is the need for this dynamic interplay between text and interpreters which we wish to emphasize. Today's readers cannot come to the text in a personal vacuum, and should not try to. Instead, they should come with an awareness of concerns stemming from their cultural background, personal situation, and responsibility to others. These concerns will influence the questions which are put to the Scriptures. What is received back, however, will not be answers only, but more questions. As we address Scripture, Scripture addresses us. We find that our culturally conditioned presuppositions are being challenged and our questions corrected. In fact, we are compelled to reformulate our previous questions and to ask fresh ones. So the living interaction proceeds (Lausanne 1978:11).

Thus our knowledge of God and His will for our lives is deepened as we grow in our understanding of His Word as it relates to our context. "Out of the context in which his word was originally given, we hear God speaking to us in our contemporary context, and we find it a transforming experience. This process is a kind of upward spiral in which Scripture remains always central and normative." (Lausanne 1978:11)

Culture is related to theology in several ways. First, culture forms the grid (or the glasses) through which man perceives the revelation of God. Communication is not simply one way, from God to man. People immersed in culture have certain perspectives and viewpoints. They see things in a particular manner.

Whenever an interpreter approaches a particular biblical text he can only approach it from his own perspective ... Thus the interpretative process involves a hermeneutical circle in which the interpreter and the text are mutually engaged and that the interpretation inevitably bears the marks of its historical context. (Stott 1979:89)

This means that culture both hinders and helps man in his understanding of God's revelation. It hinders him because his pre-understanding may deflect from or obscure his perception of what God has really said. It may help him in that "every situation makes possible a certain approach to Scripture which brings to light aspects of the message which in other situations remains less visible or even hidden." (Stott 1979:90)

Culture provides the language by which Scripture is understood and by which the Gospel is communicated. Vocabulary, syntax, figures of speech, analogies, patterns of logic and arrangement, religious and philosophical concepts and functions, all form together the medium by which a theology is conceptualized and communicated. Thus we have already seen that Bible translation is in itself a form of theologizing. Choices must be made as to the meaning of the original text. This is interpretation. Choices must be made in the way the original text is to be communicated. This is interaction with the culture. Since language is a near perfect mirror image of any given culture, the choice of language to be used in translation of the Bible involves an interaction between Gospel and Culture, between the Word of God and the world view of the people.

Context, man's culture, provides redemptive analogies by which men are enabled to understand the revelation of God. Don Richardson in **Peace Child** has demonstrated this. These analogies may be found in legends and records of the past. Or they may be found in contemporary beliefs and practices. But they are cultural road ways which lead people to an understanding of the Gospel. Thus culture can form bridges, points of contact, by which Jesus Christ is made known and real to people.

Context also poses questions for which culture demands an answer. The particular problems and emphases in a given culture may be significantly different from another culture. Since theology is meant to be the application of God's Word to man and his needs, theology is practical. It should not be imposed on the laymen by the theologians, nor should it be permanently transplanted from one culture to another. This is the reason a theology written in the west is inadequate for Africa today.

We can say that beyond dispute God has spoken to man in his culture and in a certain measure accommodated Himself to the limitations we experience. This can be seen in the Scriptures as God disclosed Himself progressively over the years to the children of Israel, then to the apostolic church in Hellenistic culture.

There can be no question that we are all culturally conditioned in the sense that we are profoundly affected by the culture in which we have been enculturated. But the problem is, to what extent is the revelation of God free to encounter man? Is God able to disclose all that He has said in Scripture to every person in every culture? When God discloses Himself to man, is this only an existential encounter without cognitive content? Does God reveal propositional truth and is this verbal truth transferable and comprehensible by all people in all cultures? Are we today able to grasp the original intention of the authors who wrote to people living in a totally different context from ours?

In brief, the question is the relationship of biblical revelation, imparted to the prophets and apostles of old, to our understanding of God's will for us in Scripture.

Biblically, we cannot separate the mighty acts of God in history from the interpretation and meaning of those events. Scripture not only records the revelatory events but the inspired meaning of those events. And God sovereignly chose the Semitic Hebrew culture through which to disclose His eternal will for all mankind. As Nicholls affirms,

> In divine wisdom God chose Abram out of a Mesopotamian culture and through his descendents formed a carrier culture that reflected the interaction of the supra-cultural content and the cultural form. Thus there is a uniqueness about the Hebrew culture of the Bible. It is not just a culture alongside any other culture, but it becomes a unique culture that carried the marks of the divine-human interaction. In the providence of God this culture was able to faithfully carry the uniqueness of the divine message of creation, sin, redemption and supremely the Incarnation and resurrection of the divine Son. (Nicholls 1979a:46)

Thus God prepared providentially a culture through which He could reveal His will for all peoples without distorting that message. The Hebrew culture became the carrier culture which was uniquely capable of receiving divine revelation without undue bias or distortion.

To what extent does our own culture distort and distend our ability to comprehend divine revelation? While culture forms the grid by which we perceive the Scriptures, that cultural grid is not so opaque that we cannot perceive the fundamental teachings of Scripture. Some suggest that all theologies are the result of cultural conditioning so that the basic explanation for the conflicting theologies in the Christian Church today is the differing cultural contexts out of which those theologies arose.

But this is a simplistic explanation. No doubt cultural dissimilation did play a part on occasions. For instance, the Reformation succeeded best among the Germanic and non-Latins who were rebelling against Roman control. Luther's own personal experience led him to find "salvation by grace through faith alone" to be the key to Christian theology. And the non-Latins in western and northern Europe embraced Reformational teaching.

But cultural dissimilation does not provide an adequate explanation for the differing theologies. Salvation by grace through faith alone is a biblical truth, amply demonstrated from the study of the Bible. And it was clearly compromised by the teachings of the Roman Church. This biblical truth has been embraced by peoples of all cultures, not by imperial decree, but by faith through the study of the Bible. Such an explanation for differing theologies ultimately leads to agnosticism, for any theology can be justified as a response to divine revelation in a given culture. Nor does it explain the fact that Christians from every culture in the world were able to assent to the Lausanne Covenant, not by coercion but freely.

Culture provides the seasoning of the food but does not change the nature of the food. We are not totally fashioned by our environment, though we are obviously influenced by it. Culture will create different emphases in theology, but will not create conflicting theologies nor change the basic thrust of Scripture.

Culture then becomes the tool by which we communicate God's Word to others. Our cultural context is the medium through which God communicates and by which we respond. But culture does not shape the meaning or message of theology. Context is a servant and not the master.

## 4. Contextualization is by the Illuminating Guidance of the Holy Spirit.

Doing theology in context is not possible without the Holy Spirit, nor is it possible by the Spirit alone. The Holy Spirit illuminates the Word, quickens the mind and empowers for living. A true response to Scripture is therefore, not possible apart from the work of the Holy Spirit. But the Spirit only works in the minds of believers and primarily through the Scriptures.

The Holy Spirit was sent by the risen Lord to lead his disciples into all truth, truth which was tied to the words of Christ (Jn. 16:13). The Holy Spirit does not speak on his own, "but whatever He hears, He will speak." The same Spirit who inspired the written Word of God (II Tim. 3:16) is the one who illuminates that

Word (I Cor. 2). Thus Scripture is the yardstick to judge whether or not an alleged insight by the Holy Spirit has divine origin or not.

## 5. Contextualization is by the Word that God has Spoken.

The "word that God has spoken" is here distinguished from the written Word of God, for it refers to that which God speaks to us through Scripture derived by the illumination of the Holy Spirit. This presupposes only a partial understanding of the total revelation. Theology contains insights that are gained through the study of the Bible. But these insights are fragmentary. This necessitates a continual return to the Word of God for correction, clarification and confirmation. The written Word of God must always judge the "word that God has spoken." For we are frequently led to conclusions which we erroneously credit to the Holy Spirit.

This principle recognizes two factors: that God speaks differently, though not conflictingly, to different people living in different contexts, and that which people profess to hear spoken to them must ever be subjected to the written Word of God.

This principle is admirably demonstrated by Andersson's study of the Lutheran church founded in Congo, Brazzaville (Andersson 1968). Andersson, a Lutheran missionary, desired to know whether the Lutheran Christians in the Congo understood the truth of justification by faith alone. Or did they depend on a salvation by works.

Andersson discovered that the Africans understood the words quite well but interpreted them differently, adapting them to their own traditional world view.

Instead of being concerned about a merciful God, these Africans were concerned about a powerful God who can secure happiness on earth. The African Christian interprets salvation in terms of good health, a long life, abundant possessions and many children. "For them salvation was not salvation of the soul, but something which made life secure here below, namely bodily health, happiness in this life, prosperity, success in all undertakings." (Andersson 1968:149)

These Christians heard the Gospel through their own cultural grid. They saw God as the powerful One who could help them in their present needs. Surely, the Bible has much to say on this subject. They heard this word because of their cultural grid.

But every word of God spoken to us existentially must be continually subjected to the authority of the written Word of God. These African Christians needed to hear that Jesus Christ is Lord who has power over all spirits. This is a biblical truth desperately needed in their context. But they also needed to hear the Word of God that salvation is by grace through faith alone, even though this concept was foreign to their culture and strange to their ears.

Therefore, we agree with those missiologists who declare that each culture forms a grid which enables people to see certain truths not so clearly understood by people in other cultures.

But we as evangelicals also insist that while culture enables men to grasp certain truths, it also blinds them from seeing other truths. And the Holy Spirit must enlighten everyone in all cultures concerning God's whole truth. The whole Bible is intended for every man. "All Scripture ... is profitable."

Therefore, we need to return repeatedly and humbly to the Scriptures to compare our understanding of what God has spoken with the written Word of God.

It would seem to me that we must distinguish between several different "words" that God speaks to us in our context. Contextualized theology includes: evangelistic theology, discipling theology and systematic theology.

As the people of God seek to proclaim the kergyma, the Gospel of Jesus Christ, they must meditate upon the Word of God with ample consideration given to their context. Evangelistic theology is the freest in structuring the approach to the people. While the Scripture remains normative, the context plays a prominent role in providing the avenues into the hearts of the people, the redemptive analogies which God can use to make the message of the Gospel lucid and gripping. Buswell speaks of this as "inculturation" (Buswell 1978b:90-93).

Discipleship theology is that teaching which believers receive. In this case the people of God seek for a deeper understanding of what God has spoken, in order to meet the needs of the believers. The questions he has, the problems he faces, all form the grid through which he searches the Scripture. God's Word is addressed to believers as they seek to have their basic needs and questions answered and as they are more firmly rooted in the faith.

Systematic theology is the all encompassing task of piecing together what God has revealed from the entire Bible. It would appear to me that the very structuring of Systematic Theology is influenced by Scripture itself. While we may focus our attention on some redemptive analogy in evangelistic theology for the purpose of communication, or while we may stress certain biblical truths pertinent to the problems faced by Christians in their walk with the Lord, systematic theology is less concerned with aspects of culture, though culture is ever the context in which we respond to Scripture. But in our attempt to bring together in some orderly fashion the full revelation of God in Scripture (and each culture has a different approach to what is considered "orderly"), it seems that the Bible is more determinative. The traditional themes of systematic theology should be treated somewhere, somehow. To organize Systematic Theology would seem to require an "orderly" progression from the doctrine of God through various doctrinal teachings of man, sin, Christ, salvation, the Church and last things. Each culture will stress differing elements and expand on certain subjects. Western theology of necessity majors on evidence for the existence of God, whereas African Christian Theology has no need to labour those points. Certainly, the format may be culturally determined. But any comprehensive treatment of what God teaches us from the Bible is largely determined by the Bible itself. God's Word sets the agenda.

## 6. Contextualization is by Living in Community and Interacting with Believers Throughout Time and Space.

Contextualizing theology is not done in the ivory tower of a classroom or library. It is not primarily an academic exercise by individuals. As the community sits together with the Word of God, there is a growing understanding of what God is saying to them in their time and space.

Koyama in his book, **Water Buffalo Theology** (1976), is a good example of how not to do theology in context. While it provides interesting reading and certainly reflects a desire to relate to the culture where he serves, it has three serious defects. First, he only plays with Scripture, without seriously grappling with the Word of God. What is needed is exegesis of the Scripture. Secondly, it is not "Buffalo" Theology, but rather a westernized version, with all sorts of ideologies learned from the West creeping into it. Ralph Covell asks this question, "Is this a product of his Asian mind, or of his ten years of American training?...I question whether this is really 'water buffalo theology.' Its very sophistication seems more appropriate for the University classroom." (Covell 1977:56) Thirdly, he fails to distinguish between natural theology and biblical theology.

Truly contextualized theology cannot be done by theologians in Geneva or Rome. Nor can it be done by men whose minds are immersed with western categories of thought and western ideologies. This means that African Christian Theology cannot evolve within a generation, though steps must be continually taken.

Each of us is sorely limited. We are finite human beings who learn slowly. Solomon observed years ago, "There is nothing new under the sun." Candid confession will reveal that original thought is slow in coming and rare as precious stones. We have all been profoundly influenced by those who have taught us. And since most of our teachers have had western origins, we cannot escape our western influence. African Christian Theology will come. But mature theological reflection that is both truly biblical and authentically African will take time.

To recognize this fact will enable us to resolve several problems. Knowing that the development of African Christian Theology is an enormous project that entails generations, we need not become frustrated at the slow pace. Furthermore, we ought not pretend that some theological contribution we may make is so original or so authentically African. Progress in theological reflection is measured by small steps, not light years.

And contrary to opinion and despite what we have already said, theology is spontaneously being contextualized in Africa through Christian hymns written to traditional melodies and rhythms, through sermons preached in churches and schools by the African believers, and through the interaction of Christians with the Word of God in their context. Wherever you have the Bible translated in the vernacular languages, you have the basis for a contextualized theology. For theology is essentially translation of the truth of God into the language of the people.

The whole issue of theology being a community affair, as they interact with believers throughout time and space, is an extremely important matter. We need to interact with Christian thought worldwide and through the 2,000 years of Christianity. This point has been placed nearer the end of the Guidelines for a purpose. If Scripture is to be normative, then it must not be obscured by theological traditions.

But African Christian Theology should not be provincial or narrow. Otherwise it becomes sectarian and ethnic. All Christian theology should be rightly related to the historic Christian affirmations of the Faith, the basic doctrines of the historic Christian Church. Peter Berger contends, "The fundamental questions of theology have been passionately considered for at least 2,000 years. It is...insufferable arrogance to think that one can begin theology in sovereign disregard of this history." (Fleming 1980:56) While evangelicals do not regard tradition, including theological affirmations of the church, on the same par with Scripture, we would be blind to ignore the past and fail to interact with the past.

The context adds the pepper and salt but it does not alter the content in such a way as to create a conflicting theology. The beauty of the Christian faith is that in spite of the hundreds of denominations and differing theological emphases, those who are truly evangelical in their faith can all ascribe to the Lausanne Covenant. There is something more that unites us than an administrative structure. We believe in one Holy Catholic Church which is united by the apostolic faith. Jesus Christ as He is revealed in Scripture, and the essential elements of the Gospel revealed in the Word of God, are the bond that brings us together. For any theology to sever that bond would be a disaster and proof of its unsound presuppositions.

## 7. Contexualization is in Their Own Language and Thought Forms.

Contextualization is pre-eminently rooted in the vernacular translation of the Word of God. That translation must be both faithful to the biblical text in Hebrew and Greek and it must convey the message with the same meaning and impact as it conveyed to the original hearers. Without translation of Scripture, you can have no contextualized theology. Therefore, translation is crucial.

Once Scripture is translated into the vernacular, theological reflection by the people is then possible, free to draw upon figures of speech, analogies, patterns of logic and arrangement, religious and philosophical concepts. Theology is proven to be contextualized by the response it evokes from the people. If the truth of Scripture is communicated by a medium which seems foreign, then it is not contextualized. If the message pierces the heart and seems like their own, then it is contextualized.

## 8. Contextualization is a Dynamic Process.

"The Word of God is living and active. Sharper than any double-edged sword, it penetrates even to dividing soul and spirit, joints and marrow; it judges the thoughts and attitudes of the heart." (Heb. 4:12)

The Word of God is living because of the active work of the Holy Spirit in bringing it alive to the people of God as they read it. As men respond to the Word, there is growth in understanding. The ultimate purpose in divine revelation is not mere information but transformation of life as people know God. Information is imparted through revelation, but the ultimate purpose is to change lives and bring men into a living knowledge of Jesus Christ. Theology therefore, ought not settle for better understanding of revelation. As the living Word interacts with the believer there is growth and development in greater commitment to God and obedience to His Word. "This radical reorientation of the whole life is the core intention of the Christian Gospel, with the informational content as instrumental and the behavioral changes as logical entailment." (Taber 1979:112)

But the dynamic nature of the Word of God means that we also come into better understanding of the will of God. The picture Paul paints in Ephesians 4 is that of being built up "until we all reach unity in the faith and in the knowledge of the Son of God and become mature, attaining to the whole measure of the fulness of Christ." The goal of theology is unity. And since theology is a dynamic process through contact with the living Word of God, interacting with an ever changing culture, ever in dialogue with the people of God living in community throughout time and space, this theology can move toward that goal established by the Apostle Paul, namely, "unity of the faith."

"Dynamic process," therefore, does not mean shifting and changing. Nor does it imply theologies that differ in their essential content. By this we mean a living relationship with Jesus Christ and His Word, so that our behaviour becomes more and more like Christ, so that our understanding of God and His will becomes more and more clear to us. "Unity of faith" is the accent of the Apostle Paul which is in contrast to the contemporary emphasis on diversity. This is not a unity forced on a people. Nor is it uniformity in every detail of theological understanding. But it is a recognition that God is One, that He has spoken in Scripture which is marked by harmony and unity, and that as the Holy Spirit leads His people into the study of Scripture there is growth, both in life and understanding.

## 9. Contextualization is for Proclamation.

Proclamation implies mission. Theology ought not be an academic discipline unrelated to life and mission. Theology is the reflection on the Word of God so that correct behaviour results. The motive of contextualization is obedience to the mission of the Church. The primary concern of the apostolic Church was not to do theology but to proclaim the Gospel faithfully to the nations in obedience to Jesus Christ. Paul was a task theologian, not a systematic theologian. But all proclamation is theological, although some preaching is better theology than others.

Proclamation is inextricably connected with the knowledge of God's Word. "How, then, can they call on the one they have not believed in? And how can they believe in the one whom they have not heard? And how can they hear without someone preaching to them?" (Rom.9:14)

Our goal as theologians, then, in seeking to contextualize our theology, is to preach the Word of God more effectively and more faithfully. The best theologians are "task theologians" who are reflecting upon the Word as they seek to proclaim the Gospel in mission.

## *END NOTE*

A substantial part of the Kikamba linguistic analysis of "time" was made by a Mukamba, Pastor Muema Joel, a former student at Scott Theological College, during a class research project. Contributing were other Akamba from Kitui, including Mwikali, Mutunga, Ngwalu, Kingoku and Thitu. Other Akamba were also consulted.

# Chapter 4

# THE PROPOSALS

As we stated in the Preface, a major purpose of this book is to challenge evangelical churches to take seriously the need to reflect upon God's revelation as it pertains to our present life with all its needs and potential. The problem usually is HOW to go about it. The MEANS often escape us. The theory of developing African Christian Theology is attractive. But the know-how and the means necessary are another thing.

The purpose of this last chapter is to present some concrete proposals. It is not our intention to suggest that these proposals are the only possible avenues of approach. There probably are as many different possible ways as there are churches and individual Christians. But if this book can only awaken evangelicals to the urgent need of becoming involved in this dynamic process of thinking through God's will for their lives in their given context, the purpose of this book will be accomplished.

Following are four suggestions as to what should be done to develop an evangelical reflection in the context of Africa.

## FIRST PROPOSAL: STATE YOUR PRESUPPOSITIONS

No one can approach the study of anything without bringing with him an array of assumptions and pre-understandings. We are all committed to some viewpoint. It is humanly impossible to approach the study of African Christian Theology without holding to certain presuppositions, for no one can be wholly free of pre-understanding in any study. For instance, if we did not presuppose the law of contradiction, no science would be possible.

Many writers claim to write with a "scientific attitude." The scientific method stresses objectivity and freedom from prejudice. This intention is excellent. But the scientific method has a serious weakness. It does not include any standard or measure which can be used in deciding truth or error. Since science cannot produce truth, truth must be imported. Therefore, many people become confused. They feel unbiased and profess objectivity. Yet they are not able to arrive at truth through the scientific method. Many times the teaching of science is a philosophy which is atheistic, materialistic and godless. In this case, science which professes to be objective, proves to be committed to a godless viewpoint.

The late Okot p'Bitek (1970) is a vivid illustration of this truth. His basic criticism of all past and present studies of African Traditional Religion is that they are not objective. He claims that they are all coloured by cultural and religious bias. Expatriates study and write on the subject with their biases. So do the African nationalists today, such as Jomo Kenyatta, Leopold Senghor, J.B. Danquah, K.A. Busia, and John Mbiti. Okot p'Bitek laments, "...instead of carrying out systematic studies of the beliefs of their peoples, and presenting them as the African peoples actually know them, African scholars, smarting under the insults from the West, claimed that African peoples knew the Christian God long before the missionaries told them about it." (1970:46) What he pleads for is "objectivity." "We must reject all forms of subjectivity, whether the subjectivity arose from anti-Christian or from pro-Christian prejudices." "...Religions must be studied and presented as accurately as possible, so as to discover the African world view." (1970:113)

In a fundamental way any valid study must be objective in the sense of being without bias or prejudice. Every scholar, especially a Christian scholar, should seek to be objective in this sense. To warp or slant the truth (the meaning of bias) is never Christian. To pre-judge the facts or to hold onto an opinion in disregard to the facts that contradict it is both unfair and unchristian.

But there are real limitations on the possibility of being objective. "Objective" also means "detached" and "impersonal." In a certain sense we need to step back and see things as they are with limited subjective involvement. There is a legitimate detachment in scholarship. But in the strict sense of the word, any scholar, whether Christian or non-Christian, is a committed person. A coldly, detached, impersonal character may describe a machine, but not a human being. "In any case," writes J.N.B. Anderson, "a complete freedom from preconceived ideas is a practical impossibility; and in my experience the unbeliever is just as much conditioned by his unbelief as the believer is by his faith." (Anderson 1970:9)

Okot p'Bitek is a case in point. While he pleads for objectivity, Ali Mazrui concludes his summary of the book by saying, "Here also is African scholarship in a mood of unabashed commitment." (p'Bitek 1970:134) A study of his book shows that p'Bitek himself approaches the subject with his own presuppositions. He assumes a liberal, higher critical viewpoint of Scripture, taking the Bible full of errors; he rejects the Christian faith and denies the existence of an infinite, eternal and personal God; he displays a total commitment to an "African thought system" and rejection of all that is "foreign," including Christianity.

He declares,

"... if the leaders sincerely believe that the social reconstruction in Africa should be based on the African world view, their religions must be studied and presented as accurately as possible, so as to discover the African world view. Christian sex ethic, its other worldliness, and its preoccupation with sin are three important areas which African intellectuals and lead-

91

ers can explore, because, here, Christianity contrasts vividly with African religions." (1970:113)

Okot p'Bitek may have desired to approach the subject with a "scientific attitude." But as Kraemer points out, "The scientific attitude in such cases is just a fancy name for personal taste." (Kraemer 1963:52) While Okot p'Bitek mentions the names of many people who wrote with bias and prejudice on the topic of African Traditional Religion, no where does he mention anyone of whom he approves. What he himself desires to do is to be objective. But what he demonstrates is that everyone, including himself, writes from a particular perspective with his own pre-understanding.

As evangelicals seeking to theologize biblically and relevantly, we need to think through those basic, fundamental assumptions which help fashion our interpretation. What all scholars need to do is to lay on the table for everyone to see the areas of pre-understanding and prior beliefs which they bring to the study. Many times disagreement with a given interpretation is not related to the facts but to the presuppositions which help fashion the interpretation of those facts. There is no data impregnated with meaning. Whatever data we handle must be given meaning and interpretation, consistent both with the facts and our world view.

Liberals structure their views of African Christian Theology, consciously or unconsciously, on the basis of prior assumptions which they take with them to their study. Evangelicals are no exception. The problem with most people, however, whatever their theological stripe may be, is that they assume that they can approach the facts with cold objectivity- "the facts are the facts", they might say.

As evangelicals we tend to follow the same pattern as others, thinking that we are simply stating the facts as they really are. The challenge being given here is for every would-be theologian to think through those assumptions with which he never really deals. They are so fundamental to all his thinking that he never has really stopped to think them through.

There are many categories of assumptions that one may want to articulate. And there are many ways one may wish to state these assumptions. In my opinion the two critical issues that need to be addressed for African Christian Theology are one's view of Scripture and of culture. For theologizing is an interaction between the Word of God and man's culture. When we think of Scripture there are two important aspects: the nature of its authority and the principles of interpretation.

Consequently, as an example of one way to declare your prior assumptions on which an evangelical theology in Africa should be built, I shall affirm my presuppositions on Biblical Authority, Biblical Interpretation and the Concept of Culture.

## Biblical Authority

The fundamental assumption which must undergird all evangelical theologizing is the belief in the full and absolute authority of all that the Bible teaches.

The Holy Scriptures composed of the Old and New Testament, are the inspired, infallible Word of God, a divine revelation to mankind, given by the plenary and verbal inspiration of the Holy Spirit (II Tim. 3:15-17; Ps. 119:89; John 10:35; Isa. 40:8). The composition of the Holy Scriptures was under the controlling inspiration of the Holy Spirit so that the written Word is both truly divine and truly human. It is truly the Word of God in that the words of Scripture teach only that which God desired to teach, each part of Scripture is marked by unity and the absence of all contradictions because the Holy Spirit is the divine author (John 17:17; II Pet. 1:21; I Pet. 1:10,11; I Cor. 2:12,13).

The Scriptures are also truly human in that inspiration did not blot out human personality. Each part of Scripture reflects the culture, experience and individuality of the human authors (cf. Luke 1:1-4). Verbal inspiration is not dictation but the supernatural and providential superintending of the writing of all canonical Scriptures, so that they are kept free from error of fact, doctrine, and judgment (Matt. 5:17,18). The Holy Scriptures are the supreme final authority for the Christian (Luke 24:27,44; Rev. 22:18,19).

This has been the historic Christian belief. During the first eight centuries of the Christian Church it is impossible to find a single doctor who disowned the plenary inspiration of Scriptures unless it was in the bosom of violent heresy (Gaussen n.d.:139). The Protestant Reformers also held to that stance. Luther declared, "Holy Scriptures cannot err." John Calvin referred to the Bible as "the pure Word of God, the infallible rule of His holy truth" (Tenney 1960:24).

## Biblical Interpretation

Biblical hermeneutics is the second focal point of our presuppositions. Like the question of biblical authority, the science and art of interpreting the Scriptures is being undermined by a subjectivity comparable to the subjective emphasis in divine revelation by the neo orthodox.

As evangelicals we believe that the interpretation of Scripture is based both on objective and subjective principles: the objective nature of God's revelation and the subjective nature of man's comprehension of that revelation.

The Bible communicates divine truth for all peoples in objective propositional statements. The goal of the exegete is to ascertain from the biblical text what the primary meaning of the author was and so intended for his readers. The meaning of Scripture is not derived from the interpreter's context or experience, but from the Scripture itself. What the Bible teaches is relevant to all peoples everywhere, whether they comprehend that relevance or not. It is God's Word to man and man's response must be obedience. To interpret the Bible we must seek the normal sense of those propositions. Grammatico-Historical exegesis is basic in which the words are understood in the linguistic and historical context. Literal interpretation is the opposite of allegorical. We seek to interpret the Scriptures in the normal way we interpret any literary writing. All figures of speech and literary forms are recognized.

93

Since the Holy Spirit is the Divine Author of the 66 canonical books, the Scriptures are marked by unity. Progressive revelation means that greater light and understanding were granted to God's people through the passing of the centuries. But inspiration ensures that there is harmony among all the parts. Thus later revelation helps to interpret earlier revelation; the Old Testament is interpreted in the light of the New Testament. Scripture interprets Scripture. The best interpreter of Scripture is the Scripture itself for God is the Author of all of it.

The second aspect of biblical hermeneutics is the subjective nature of man's comprehension of that revelation. The Holy Spirit who inspired the prophets and apostles to write His Word, also illuminates His people as they read it. Only those who are born of the Spirit and made members of the Body of Christ possess the Holy Spirit. Only He can lead His people into a true understanding of what God has spoken.

These two aspects, the objective nature of biblical revelation and the subjective nature of man's comprehension must be both maintained. Personal meaning and application are derived by an individual as he searches out the Bible for himself. But his subjective understanding is always held in check by the objective propositional nature of biblical revelation. The Holy Spirit today cannot contradict what He taught in the Bible. When Christians disagree on what the Bible teaches, they must continually return to the Scriptures in order to have their own minds and understanding reformed. Neither propositional revelation nor the illumination of the Holy Spirit can be eliminated. Both are essential.

## Concept of Culture

We suggest that a third category of assumptions which ought to be considered by those seeking to develop African Christian Theology is the question of man's culture.

Culture is the life way of a people, the totality of what man has learned, the social legacy he passes on to his children. Culture therefore includes the external objects which he creates and the internal meaning and order he gives to the world. As such, culture is the creation of man and a reflection of himself in his own historical and geographical context.

Following are the affirmations we make concerning the nature of culture based on our understanding of Scripture.

### 1. Culture as such is ordained by God from creation.

God created man and woman so that society would be born and culture would be developed. Through culture God is pleased to communicate. In this sense, Christ is **for** culture.

### 2. Culture since the Fall is corrupted by sin.

The effects of sin on culture are analogous to the effects of sin on man. Every part of culture is affected by man's sinful bent away from God and on himself. The world view by which man interprets and understands the world is perverted by sin. His values, customs and habits are marked by rebellion against God. In this sense, Christ is **against** culture.

94

**3. Because man continues to be born in the image of God (albeit, a fallen image) and confronted with the revelation of God in nature and conscience, man's culture can serve adequately to communicate the Gospel.**

Each culture has true insights into reality. Redemptive analogies can be used to communicate the Gospel. God's Word can be comprehended by the illumination of the Holy Spirit because every man lives in God's world which He has not abandoned. In this sense, Christ is pleased to communicate **through** culture.

**4. The Gospel has been revealed by God for the purpose of transforming people and their culture.**

Some parts of culture may be adapted for the glory of God while other parts must be rejected. Most of culture may be preserved but must be transformed to agree more perfectly with the Word of God. In this sense, Christ **transforms** culture.

**5. Because mankind is created in the image of God and descended from one father and mother, God is able to communicate His will through the Scriptures to every culture.**

The Bible contains teaching which applies to every culture. Though God's revelation was given through the Hebrew and Greek cultures, that message can be comprehended by people of all cultures. God is able to communicate the Gospel through the Bible to people in every culture because the whole human race is one in their origin and nature. Through the study of Scripture, the Body of Christ continues to grow into the unity of the faith (Eph. 4:13).

African Christian Theology can only be evangelical if the basic presuppositions are evangelical. Evangelical theology cannot grow from liberal roots. The first task in developing an evangelical theology is to ensure that the basic pre-understanding is evangelical.

# SECOND PROPOSAL: ORGANIZE YOUR PLAN FOR THEOLOGICAL REFLECTION

Most frequently the pattern for theologizing is for some individual scholar, employed as a professor in a university or theological college, to take up his pen and compose a book on some theological subject. This is surely one possibility. But in that case it represents the opinion of one individual.

In our Guidelines for contextualizing theology we suggested that such work should be done by the living community of the people of God, interacting with believers throughout time and space. There is good reason to believe that this is an appropriate approach for the churches of Jesus Christ in Africa today.

In the first place, the traditional pattern in Africa for doing anything is to do it in community. Decisions are made by the community and not by an individual. Applied to the context of the Body of Christ, the Christian Church is the New Community. We suggest that each particular branch of the Christian Church in Africa (each Christian denomination) should embrace the task of theologizing. Developing an African Christian Theology should not be the work of individuals without appropriate relationship with their churches. Rather, each Christian church should decide together WHAT and HOW they will engage in the holy task of seeking God's will for their lives as it pertains to various questions they face.

In the second place, enlisting the contributions of many of God's people will contribute toward the growth of the whole Body of Christ. One purpose of developing African Christian Theology is to help the Christian church to grow in her knowledge of God and His will for their lives; and more, to grow in her obedience to that will. The more Christians we enlist in the task of thinking through the issues from a biblical perspective, the more likely we will make an impact on the whole Christian Church.

Another reason for promoting a communal reflection upon God's Word is the need to find the necessary resources required to do the work. Generally speaking, church leaders are over-worked. The thought of adding to their job description another task is not very welcome. Those most capable are the busiest, very often. By enlisting many people to participate in this work, we will help to distribute the responsibilities.

With these preliminary thoughts in mind, we propose the following organizational structure. At first it may appear rather complicated. The proposal is only one of many that could be offered. Nevertheless, this proposal has much to be commended and in fact is in use in various circles.

## 1. The Church Approves a Theological Advisory Group.

Somehow the official approval of the church leadership needs to be sought before any theologizing can have pervasive impact within the churches. Each denomination, organized on different lines, will need to seek their own particular avenue of achieving this objective.

The manner in which each Christian denomination may achieve this purpose will vary from church to church. However, the objective should be the same, namely, the official involvement of the church body so that the Christian churches can pass judgment on all theologizing, and so that all theological reflection can benefit the whole church down to the grass roots level.

## 2. The Theological Advisory Group should research various needs.

This will be discussed in greater detail later on. But the principle should be stated here. The Christian Church in Africa faces various unique problems that have not been carefully reflected on in the light of God's Word. Whether they relate to traditional problems such as polygamy and circumcision, or whether they relate to contemporary issues such as the proper use of money, God's people need to search the Scripture to know what He is saying to His people in this given context. Therefore, prior to any study of Scripture there must be exploration of the nature of those needs.

We might give as one example of how this can be done, the seminars conducted by Dr. John Gration. In 1984 Dr. John Gration of the Wheaton College Graduate School conducted several seminars in Zaire and Kenya with representatives coming from other countries. These three day seminars were limited to about 15 participants each in order to facilitate interaction. All the participants had considerable church experience so that they could contribute from their knowledge of the people with whom they worked. "Gospel and Culture" was the subject. No lectures were given. Instead, the attempt was to draw out of the participants their understanding of the Gospel and Culture and to help them think of ways in which the Gospel had brought changes to their culture, and ways in which more change needed to be made.

One need not depend upon expertise from abroad to help us think through our particular needs. By convening a small group of knowledgeable and experienced persons within the churches, somewhere between ten to twenty in number, you can explore together the whole question of the urgent needs which require resolution through the application of God's Word.

Whether this research into needs is done with individuals or in groups, there should be a concerted effort to discover those deep needs which the Christian Church should address. One advantage of meeting with a group is that interaction stimulates more thought and may lead to more creative thinking.

### 3. The Theological Advisory Group should meet to plan.

a. Those felt needs obtained by research with knowledgeable groups of people should be prioritized. Since we cannot tackle all of them at once, a few should be chosen to research. Since we usually learn by our mistakes, it may be well to choose only one or two needs for research and consider this a pilot project for experimentation. Having learned by our mistakes in the pilot project, we can plan better for the further development of our theological reflection.

b. The Theological Advisory Group (TAG) should then appoint a Research Team of 3-5 individuals or more.

The selection of the Research Team is crucial. Each member of the team should have a careful knowledge of the Word of God and extensive experience in church ministry. They should be known and respected by the churches. One might suggest that ideally, they should all have graduate level training in a seminary or theological college, though in practice this may be impossible. But one could also argue that to produce theological reflection we need to reflect all levels of thought down to the grass roots. Theologizing that is theoretical without practical relevance is useless. Theology that cannot be communicated to the illiterate lay person is sorely wanting. Therefore, one might desire to enlist a wide range of skills on the Research Team, representing various areas of speciality, including some lay persons from the grass roots of the churches. Thus the Reseach Team is composed of individuals with a variety of experience and expertise so that they can compliment one another.

The key individual on the Research Team is the Manuscript Drafter who is the Chairman of the Research Team. It is essential that whatever level of education the other members of the Research Team may have obtained, the Manuscript Drafter ought to have an earned Bachelor of Divinity degree (or the M.Div. equivalent) and have demonstrated his writing and research skills at a professional level. For in the end he is the one to fashion and shape the piece of research into a written document.

## 4. The Research Team engages in research.

a. The Research Team always works together as a team. They strategize and plan together, though they may as individuals carry out their research in their own given areas. So they will need to meet periodically to plan and review.

b. Thorough field research must first be made into the exact nature and extent of the problem before them. If the subject is polygamy, then investigation should be made into the various ways in which this has proved to be a problem in the churches. Examples and illustrations may be gathered. Speak to both the polygamists concerned and the church leaders concerned. Before we can know God's will concerning the Christian way of handling polygamy, we need to make penetrating investigation into the nature of the problem.

The more research, the better. This applies to all field research. We need to be resourceful in finding ways of securing the necessary people to do the work without unnecessary expenses.

One possible solution is to teach Field Research in all our pastoral training institutions. Equip the Bible School and Bible College students with a know-how to do field research. Then use these students to assist in making inquiry. Our research should not be restricted to one small locality. If we use people located in different parts of the church constituency to do research for us, we have a better chance of making adequate research.

Another possible solution is a wise structuring of our Bible Schools and Colleges. Who else are the more likely candidates to give leadership in the developing of theological study than our teachers in Bible Schools and Theological Colleges? They are the ones whose lives are devoted (hopefully) to the study of God's Word to help future church workers understand God's Word as it pertains to our lives.

If the theological colleges would cooperate with the goals of the Theological Advisory Group, participating with TAG whole heartedly in developing African Christian Theology, they could assist greatly. If a particular teacher is selected by TAG to assist in the research of a particular topic, the school could assign him to teach an elective course on that topic. If that teaching assignment were made well in advance, the teacher could devote himself over the holidays to research and develop his course. Through interaction with the students he would be sharpened in his understanding of the problem and biblical perspective. In this way the teacher is killing two birds with one stone. He is teaching a course in the theological college and at the same time developing his understanding of the research project for TAG.

Another venturesome possibility is the institution of one-term sabbaticals for the specific purpose of research for the Theological Advisory Group. Teachers need to be refreshed like everyone else. If they continue to teach the same materials year after year, they will grow stale and irrelevant. Many universities and colleges overseas have found this a necessity to help up-grade their teachers. And in the process of upgrading the teachers they up-grade the institution. The quality of the college is no higher than the quality of the teachers. So as they assist their teachers to grow and develop personally, they also assist their own schools to grow and develop. Our recommendation is that serious consideration be given to the development of short sabbaticals (preferably of three month duration) with one specific purpose of assigning them the responsibility of research for the Theological Advisory Group.

No doubt the sabbaticals would need careful thought and stringent regulations. These three month sabbaticals are not holidays. Nor are they occasions of reduced pressure from work. They are opportunities to study and research in preparation for developing evangelical theology in Africa.

Remember! African Christian Theology, as is true of theology done anywhere, requires hard work. If we settle for shallow research, our results will be superficial. The only solution to quality theology is in-depth research and extended research. The Research Team will need to find resourceful ways of enlisting the help of others to research for them or with them in order to multiply their effectiveness.

c. Thorough study of the Scriptures should then be made in an effort to discern God's answer to this felt need. For this reason the Research Team needs to have more than a basic knowledge of the Bible. At the very least, the Manuscript Drafter should have a working knowledge of Greek and Hebrew and access to Bible study tools. The Research Team may also make use of other personnel, expert in biblical studies, to assist them.

It is assumed that the Research Team will consider carefully the underlying theological causes for the problem being studied. The problem tackled may be only the obvious symptom of some deeper, less obvious underlying root problem or problems. The Research Team has the responsibility of exploring these root problems and developing a biblical answer to those problems.

Most problems are complex, not simple. In the same way, God's perspective on that problem is probably complex with many different angles. We need to search the whole Scriptures, always remembering that New Testament revelation helps us to interpret the Old Testament. Biblical study on the problem should include secondary sources, that is, biblical studies and conclusions by other theologians. But it is essential that above all else, primary attention be given to the biblical text itself.

Mature, seasoned thought comes through a prayerful study of the Scriptures and interaction with others over a period of time. It is amazing what the Holy Spirit can do in our subconscious minds when we earnestly reflect on His Word over an extended period of time. To interact with other believers, sharing our thoughts, learning from them, all helps us to develop a mature, well balanced Christian perspective.

d. Further research is done in the field, possibly with consultative groups, to enquire into the possible African Christian solution to the problem before us. Various knowledgeable and articulate individuals from the grass roots level are gathered together to think through the problem and to communicate the biblical perspective on that issue. Through field research various proverbs, traditions, examples, stories, and analogies are gathered which help us to make the final results truly African in nature.

e. After a given period of time the Research Team collates the data gained and drafts an outline of the problem and biblical response.

f. The Manuscript Drafter must then compose a full report, incorporating all the material gathered.

g. With this document in hand the Research Team then consults with several Resource Groups. A Resource Group is a select group of people in the field with a good knowledge and experience of the subject at hand. Prior to the meeting with them, the full report written by the Manuscript Drafter is sent to each member of the Resource Group for private reading and consideration.

During the day long meeting with the Resource Group, with one or more members of the Research Team, enquiry is made into the adequacy of the Full Report. Do they agree with the way the problem or need has been presented? Are they satisfied with the adequacy of the biblical response? What is their reaction to the cultural relevance of the format and content for communicating most effectively?

Remember! The object is to produce a thoroughly biblical and an authentically African solution to the problem before us. The purpose of the meetings with the Resource Groups is to gain feed back from them. What further insights do they have? Is the full report adequate? Is it on target? Is it presented most effectively?

h. On the basis of this further in-put from the Resource Groups, the Manuscript Drafter then compiles the revised theological statement (the generic report), taking into account all the contributions that have been made. He is at liberty to discriminate and reject some ideas. But such rejected ideas should be compiled at the end of the report in an addendum, so as not to lose them. For in the end the Theological Advisory Group will have the final say, for the final results are by consensus.

## 5. Theological Advisory Group considers the full report.

a. The Theological Advisory Group is first given the full report in writing for private reading and consideration.

b. As the Theological Advisory Group meets together they evaluate the strengths and weaknesses of the Full Report, making possible recommendations for further revision-

-either need for further biblical research,

-and/or a need for more culturally relevant ways of theologizing

-adequacy of the theological understanding of the root causes, not only the surface symptom.

Remember! Our goal is to be thoroughly biblical and authentically African. This is to be African Christian Theology in the best of evangelical tradition.

Remember, also! "People learn from one another, just as iron sharpens iron." (Prov. 27:17 TEV) So the more we consult, the more insights we may obtain. And the insights we are seeking pertains to two aspects of our study: a thorough study of the biblical perspective on the subject, and an authentically African way of thinking through and communicating that biblical perspective.

c. Whatever recommendations the Theological Advisory Group will make, it is the responsibility of the Research Team to complete the Full Report in accordance with those recommendations. For the Theological Advisory Group has the final authority in the production of the theological report.

d. The Theological Advisory Group must then consider the target population. To whom should we address our contextualized Bible study?

The Full Report (a generic theological statement) represents the research done in both the biblical and contextual aspects of the problem. But it does not represent our final goal. The Theological Advisory Group may find it desirable to publish the generic report. Perhaps a series of publications could be envisioned so that the hard work and notable achievement can be used by others. However, this is not our final goal.

In any communication we must determine the target population. To whom should we address the biblical response?

For example, if we are studying the problem of separation and divorce in our churches, to whom should we address the Word of God? To the pastors who give pre-marital counselling? To the youth in youth camps and elsewhere before marriage? To the engaged couple who receives pre-marital counselling? To the parents and older members of the family who also give counsel to the engaged?

We desire an integrated approach which applies biblical studies to all the relevant groups involved. Instead of developing a generalized Bible Study for everyone (which is what the generic report is), we need to think specifically of the various target populations who need to be addressed if any change is to come about.

e. The Theological Advisory Group then considers what MEANS can best be used to communicate the Word of God on this topic to the various target populations. Such means may include the following:

AGENCIES- such as Bible studies, pastor's conferences, Bible School courses, seminars for laymen, youth camps, Theological Education by Extension, Christian Education Department, pulpit preaching, Christian Youth Fellowship etc.

TOOLS- what kind of tools are needed for communicating through each agency? - such as Bible study guides, programmed instruction materials for

101

T.E.E., materials and suggestions for conducting a conference or seminar, teacher's and/or pastor's notes.

PROCEDURES- how do we go about encouraging and promoting the communication of this message from God's Word? Much valuable research lies unused, lost in the files, the libraries, and the committee minutes. We need to work on this aspect of communicating with the churches what God has spoken to us in our research.

## 6. The Research Team develops the tools designated by TAG.

Once the tools have been developed, they are tested in the field. Consultative Resource Groups are presented with the proposed materials with the intention of learning from them how effective they are and where they can be improved.

Are they relevant to the culture?

Are they accurate in their total perspective?

Are they effective in communicating?

The Manuscript Drafter is responsible to draft the tools, though the Research Team makes their contribution. Any difference with that which has been written by the Manuscript Drafter is resolved by consensus, through talking out the differences and coming to an agreement.

## 7. The Theological Advisory Group meets once again.

The final approval for the tools is made by TAG through consultation, before they are all given to the church governing body which appointed the members of TAG in the first place.

Through consultation with the church governing body, the Theological Advisory Group appoints field personnel to begin implementing the use of the tools prepared. In many ways this is the most critical stage. Many valuable materials have been produced which lie dormant and unused. Unless we can find ways and means of stimulating the churches to use these materials, we shall fail in our primary goal.

However simple or complex our research plan may be, we need to remember, there are no short cuts. If we want QUALITY theological study, we must invest much time and effort. While we should enlist a large number of people in theological reflection, the Manuscript Drafter in addition to church ministry experience ought to have graduate training in biblical or theological study and be a proven scholar and capable writer.

# THIRD PROPOSAL: RESEARCH
# THE CRUCIAL NEEDS

The third proposal is that we thoughtfully investigate the crucial needs in our context that need a biblical resolution.

We have already noted that one of the first projects in developing African Christian Theology is to investigate the crucial needs for which we must find God's answer. The list of felt needs is a long one and differs in differing contexts.

When exploring the various needs we should think of the wide spectrum. For our present needs include those rooted in our past traditions and those arising from contemporary developments; they involve both personal piety and social concerns. Needs which require theological reflection are found both in the organized churches and in society as a whole. Wherever men and women are functioning, there you will find crucial needs. What does God say about the Christian answer to those needs? That is the challenge before us.

To help stimulate our thoughts, let me cite some possible crucial needs.

## Needs Rooted in our Traditional Past

There are various needs which are rooted in our past traditions and which have not been adequately thought through biblically. At least there is need for the African Christian churches today to reflect upon these in the light of God's Word because there are continuing problems in these areas.

The problem of polygamy and the baptism of polygamists continually surfaces in various councils. What should the Christian Church require of a polygamist when he is converted to Jesus Christ in the state of polygamy? Many times if a baptized monogamist marries a second wife, he simply transfers to another denomination which accepts him into membership. Because of a poor state of church discipline in most churches and because they frequently compete for members, Christians may simply play games with the churches. It would be desirable, though perhaps an impossible dream these days, if evangelical churches could take a common stand on some of these issues leading to church discipline.

Witchcraft is a growing problem among many churches with Christians seeking help from the medicine man (the traditional shaman who communicates with the spirit world). Dreams are relied upon by many Christians for guidance in making decisions. Male and female circumcision still surface as unresolved problems. What should our attitude be toward brideprice?

These and a host of other crucial problems prevail which have their roots in traditional culture. Today the African evangelical churches are called upon to reflect upon these and offer guidance and direction to the Christian struggling with these problems.

## Needs of Contemporary Origin

There is a growing problem of separation and divorce today, even among Christians. This problem was not prevalent in the African past and is no doubt related to the whole break down of the family and traditional culture. Since the

Christian churches (and missions) contributed toward the break-down of traditional culture, we have a responsibility of restoring stability to the family, that foundational unit of every society. For whenever the family deteriorates, society will also disintegrate. What word from God does the Christian Church in Africa receive today concerning family life and the integrity of the family?

A sampling of other needs of contemporary origin include: corruption and the wrong handling of money; a growing problem of crime, unknown in traditional Africa as it is today; the question of family planning and birth control.

## Needs in the Churches

There is a tragic lack of biblical knowledge among believers. Because of a shallow and superficial knowledge of the Word of God, moral and organizational problems often develop. Situations arise in which people do not know how to deal with them biblically.

A growing problem of nominalism is prevalent in the churches. Because Christianity is now the culturally accepted belief of a large number of Africans, people are baptized and enter church membership without being born again. Hence we find a common distinction made between the Christian and the saved.

In many churches there is inadequate worship. In the face of dying traditions which provided opportunities for fellowship, Sunday morning services are more social in emphasis than worshipful. The idea of worshipping God with reverence is absent. Absence of worship is in many cases tied to a lack of spiritual vitality among both pastors and elders who lead the service.

Church leadership is frequently corrupt. There is a power craze in the churches with political style campaigns and struggles for leadership. The pastors and church leaders think of their authority in terms of political leadership. They become authoritative. Once a ruling is made, no one can challenge it.

There is a frequent gap between the church leaders and the laity. Leaders make policy decisions while the members are distant. The laity give their money but there is no acountability of money received. When leaders do not communicate fully with the people, the laity can become inactive and unwilling to contribute much. There needs to be greater unity between the leaders and laity through accountability, particularly in the area of finance. Misappropriation of money by the church leaders is the result.

Because African Christian Theology is first of all concerned about the rule of the Kingdom of God in the churches, it is only natural that most of the crucial problems which trouble the Christian community are in the churches. This list could be extended at great length.

Many Christian churches are weak on church discipline. Christians including elders sin but they are not properly disciplined. They may be removed from office without dealing with the problem openly. Then they are returned to office for unknown reasons in the future. Pastors may misappropriate funds but there is no discipline, only the deduction of some money from their monthly salary.

There is the problem of legalism, judging people on the basis of external, extra-biblical standards. For instance, in some circles there is a battle of words. If one does not say, "Praise the Lord" or "Brother" so and so, he is judged to be un-spiritual as a Christian. Wearing certain styles of clothing is judged to be sinful, not because of morality but because of differences.

Other critical problems in many churches include absence of prayer and Bible study, lack of powerful preaching, lack of a biblical concept of stewardship, improper methods of fund raising, compromise at funerals when the messages are given which imply a hope for the dead if we pray for the dead, the lack of proper emphasis and understanding of Holy Communion and a dichotomy between Christian profession and practice.

## Needs in Society

My own personal conviction is that the Christian Church's first responsibility is to set her own house in order. We ought to be concerned about social sins and have the courage to speak out against them. But if Jesus Christ is not exercising his lordship among His people in the churches, we are in a very weak position to exercise a prophetic role in society. If the Christian Church is a spiritual, dynamic body which reflects the holiness of God, then her voice in society will commend attention. Let us give priority to the dynamic work of the Holy Spirit within the churches through powerful preaching and prayer. As God sanctifies His people wholly, we are then capable of being the light and salt in the world to which God has called us.

Many social ills can only be resolved through the Gospel of Jesus Christ. Lack of justice is a serious crime, particularly when the poor and minorities are oppressed by the rich elite. The Bible has much to say about justice and equity among all peoples. Tribalism often enters into this problem whereby people are employed at work or acquited in a court because of ethnic origins.

Drunkenness and sexual immorality are social problems. Advocates of birth control are teaching children the use of contraceptives as young as eight years of age. This is not family planning but license for immorality. The Roman Catholic Church opposes all artificial means of birth control. Articles are written in the newspapers advocating various philosophies. Have we thought through from a bi-blical perspective what advice we should offer to Christians today?

## Doctrinal Problems

There is such confusion among many people today concerning the Person and work of the Holy Spirit. Through neglect on the one hand and through mis-guided zeal on the other hand the biblical teaching concerning the ministry of the Holy Spirit and His gifts is woefully misunderstood. Evangelicals as a group and in their various denominational circles must think through biblical revelation lest we become further fragmented and divided over this biblical doctrine.

Our young people in their schools are being taught evolution, atheism, humanism, universalism, Marxism and the denial of hell. These are not traditional African beliefs. Nor are they biblical. What help are our churches giving to our youth who struggle with these issues with teachers of Christian Religious Education who know not God nor His Word and who are poor models for the youth?

In fact the evangelical Christian churches must give serious thought to a wide range of doctrinal issues. Not only should they reflect on these problems but they should reflect upon the whole of biblical revelation from an African perspective in order to possess the Christian Faith as their very own. If this is done with full confidence in the Bible and with an authentic African perspective, the result will automatically be Christian theology done in the context of Africa and with an African stamp upon it.

## FOURTH PROPOSAL: ESTABLISH YOUR GOALS

Why should the evangelical Christian churches be engaged in such a tedious process of theologizing when in fact there are millions of people outside the churches who need to be evangelized? Historically, the evangelicals have primarily stressed evangelism with little attention given to theological reflection. The result is obvious today. How many evangelical theologians and biblical scholars are found within our universities? How many evangelicals are leading people in discussion and research of theological issues and publishing their research? Despite the fact that the vast majority of Protestants are evangelical at the grass roots level in Africa today, there are a pitiful few who are sufficiently trained and well placed so that they are able to give leadership to develop an evangelical theology for the African context.

What the Christian churches need to realize is that if this pursuit of theologizing is done with proper goals, it will help us to accomplish exactly what we are so deeply concerned about, namely, a revitalized, renewed church which is growing through evangelistic outreach.

One example from the history of the Africa Inland Mission may bring this point home to us. The A.I.M. was founded specifically for evangelism. As stated in the first constitution of 1902, "The object shall be evangelization in Inland Africa, as God shall direct." (A.I.M. 1902: Constitution)

Through the course of the years a struggle developed between evangelism and education. At first schools were a means of presenting the Gospel to the students and the A.I.M. gladly entered the field of education. But during the period of 1920 through 1945 the Christians began to clamour for more and more schools. "As the Christian community increased, education began to outgrow its avowedly evangelistic beginnings." (Oliver 1966:212) Hence the A.I.M. developed an ambivalence toward education. This reluctance to meet the felt needs of education by the African Christians in the Africa Inland Church became one of the chief sources of contention between the mission and the church. Because of an outright crisis that developed, the A.I.M. changed its policy in 1945 and began a crash programme of opening a minimum of 20 secondary schools in four years.

The irony is this. Gration argues that "a history of the Mission's educational program is in a real sense a history of the growth of the Church. The Church grew out of the school room; in fact, this is where it was born. For better or worse, Church and school in the early days were practically synonymous." (Gration 1974:156) During those periods when the A.I.M. placed significant emphasis on education, the churches grew the most rapidly.

In the same manner I believe that if we devote proper attention to biblical study and reflection upon God's Word as it pertains to our contemporary situation, we shall find that the result will be spiritual renewal in the churches and greater church growth—at least, quality growth with genuine conversions.

But for that to happen we must establish proper goals. What is our primary purpose in developing African Christian Theology? Is it to affirm our identity? Is it to compete with the liberals? Is it to publish books and magazine articles? Is it to give "correct" answers to people's questions? All these goals fall far short of anything worthy of the great effort required to develop an evangelical theological reflection.

As we seek to glorify God in everything we do, our chief purpose in theologizing should be spiritual renewal. Theologizing apart from changed lives is a useless endeavour. Yes, it is even dangerous. We may have an appearance of doing a good work, but in the eyes of God our theologizing is not complete. And though we may have a name that we are live, active Christians, God declares that we are "dead" spiritually (cf. Rev. 3:1).

For many years I rejected the very words, "theology" and "theologian." For they communicated to me something in which I did not believe. If theology is an academic exercise, it is of limited value. If theologians are elite academicians who speculate and theorize, we ought not seek to be one.

But theology like Christian Education is related to life. The purpose of Christian Education is not the imparting of facts. We have not taught unless lives are changed. Nor have we reflected properly upon divine revelation unless our lives are changed. Thus the primary purpose of theologizing should always be to become more and more like Jesus Christ and to become more obedient to His will in all things.

With this in mind I propose that **our primary goal in developing an African Christian Theology should be spiritual renewal among the churches and the building up of the Kingdom of God.**

Along with all the organizational arrangements mentioned above in developing a carefully researched theology, we need to promote prayer for revival. Our purpose is not simply to develop a theological statement and tools for use. Our purpose is nothing less than changed lives. And this cannot be done apart from the work of the Holy Spirit. Our whole task of theological research must be bathed in prayer. But more than that, the communication of the Word of God to the peoples, from the grass roots level to the top leadership, must be saturated with prayer. Our deepest concern is to see God move among His people to bring them into a greater conformity to the life of our Lord Jesus Christ. Our deepest concern is to see the reign of Christ among us so that God's will is being done on earth as it is in heaven.

Revival has always come through intensive prayer and in the study of God's Word. Prayer alone does not bring revival. But as men seek the face of God in prayer and are confronted with the will of God as disclosed in Scripture, God is pleased many times to visit His people. This is our longing and prayer. For we are not seeking merely the publication of materials, even good, evangelical biblical studies, as worthwhile as they may be. We are looking for changed lives by beholding the Saviour.

We began this book with a quotation from John Mbiti "Christianity has Christianized Africa, but Africa has not africanized Christianity." It is an open question to what extent Christianity has Christianized Africa. And it is equally debatable whether Africa has not to any extent africanized Christianity. Perhaps it would have been less graphic but more accurate to state that Christianity has to some extent Christianized Africa but Africa has not fully africanized Christianity.

We may conclude our book with three observations.

## Africanized Christianity- A Living Reality

It is our contention that to some extent the Christian faith has been africanized. Contextualization has in fact been taking place. African believers are making their unique imprint on the Christian faith in the continent. And this has been done spontaneously and naturally as Christians have sought to express their faith through their own culture.

Perhaps an illustration from Kitui among the Akamba could demonstrate the point.

Birth traditionally is a time of rejoicing and a time of grave concern for the life of the baby since infant mortality was very high. Certain traditions developed which helped to ensure the safety of the baby and to incorporate the young one into the family. These traditions were known as **ndua.**

Spontaneously, the Body of Christ has evolved Christian adaptations. Various Christians among the Akamba in Kitui have developed the custom of joining together with the Christian family to rejoice and pray. They kill a goat, eat together, rejoice and sing. The women bring presents for the child, gourds filled with porridge, tea leaves and sugar. This is often done during the time of naming the child. The traditional custom among the Akamba which is the counterpart of the Christian practice is called **ndua** at which time they would celebrate the whole night with dancing and drinks. The Christian functional substitute is an opportunity for believers to rejoice together and share their concern for the little one. Prayer is offered specifically for the health and physical well being of the infant.

This kind of ceremony flourishes in some areas but is absent in others. The origins of this functional substitute are obscure, though it seems to have been spontaneous. Much of the genuine contextualizing of the Gospel is indeed spontaneous, arising from the grass roots level as Christians seek to live out their faith.

The constituent elements of this functional substitute are truly African- feasting, merry making, communal sharing, and prayer for the security and health of the child. Herein lies the strength of the Christian Church in Africa. The community of believers demonstrating their solidarity with one another during important events with a conscious dependence upon God and His presence and power among them. You can look high and low in the western world and fail to find anything similar to that which has just been described.

We contend that the process of contextualizing the gospel has in fact been taking place in many places and in various ways. Not only have various spontaneous practices developed which reflect the African context, but the thought life of the church to some extent has been marked by the African culture.

However, the plain fact is that much more can and should be done. During the past century africanizing the Christian faith was done in limited ways. But the call for evangelicals today is to procede with the task of reflecting upon God's Word in the African context with the purpose of allowing Jesus Christ to be Lord of His Church. "THY Kingdom come, THY will be done on earth as it is in heaven."

The local congregations of believers would greatly benefit their fellow members if efforts were made to think through natural ways of expressing their faith in the African context. How can Christianity Christianize traditional rites of birth, initiation, and marriage? How can Jesus Christ be made Lord of every aspect of life, during planting season, harvest, times of sickness and death? While Christianity has been in the process of being africanized for many years, we would do well to continue the process with conscious and intentional efforts to enable the multiplying millions of African Christians to communicate their faith in Jesus Christ more effectively and to worship their Lord more naturally.

## Africanized Theology- Built on the Bible

To invite Jesus Christ to be our Lord necessitates His rule by His Word in our lives, both judging and saving. A major emphasis in these pages has been the absolute primacy of the written Word of God for evangelical theologizing.

Many lament the superficiality of Christianity in Africa, laying the blame wholly on our failure to contextualize the Gospel. Whatever truth may lie in that assertion, we would argue rather that the weakness in African Christianity is due to two problems: a nominal Christianity without true conversion and the new birth, and a tragic famine of the teaching of the Bible so that those people who are genuinely saved are not properly instructed in the Word of God.

A strong case can be made that Christians lapse into their traditional religion because they are weak in faith and this weak faith is due to a lack of biblical teaching. The problem is not necessarily that Christianity is not africanized but that people are not born again, though they call themselves Christians. And the problem is that born again believers are not taught the Word of God sufficiently to enable their faith to grow firm. Why is it that many African believers are not troubled by their traditional religion such as the ancestral cult? Why is it that there are so many fine, mature, consistent, Christ-like Christians in Africa? How have they succeeded in africanizing Christianity, if that is the major problem? What is so desperately needed in our churches is clear, dynamic and powerful preaching and teaching of God's Word so that the Holy Spirit can change lives. Several illustrations may be helpful.

Mary was 40 years old, deeply engrossed in traditional religion, ready to become a diviner, possessing all the equipment necessary. But she was troubled by her ancestral spirits. Daily she was plagued by them, finding no rest or peace from them. At night time they would appear to her and choke her. In the process of becoming a diviner, she was attacked by them. She was informed that her problems were due to the displeasure of her ancestors. She did not enjoy health because of them.

During the course of these problems her son-in-law died. The Christians from the Africa Inland Church came to comfort her and gave a Christian witness. The Gospel witness lingered in her mind. She later went to the A.I.C. church where Musango and another elder led her to the Lord.

Since then she has never been troubled by the ancestors. They ceased to disturb her. She believes that the reason some other Christians return to the medicine man in times of crisis is that they are not taught properly from the Word of God. Whenever calamity comes, the traditional approach is to visit the medicine man and ask WHY, seeking protection from any further attack. Christians must be taught the power of God so they will not fear, she says. Mary has never felt a need to go back to the medicine man.

What is her secret? Besides being born again, prayer is her support. Friends come to her home and they pray together when trouble comes. Sometimes she sends for the elders of the church to visit her in times of need. Christians pay her a visit several times in a year just to rejoice together in the Lord and pray together. She attends church weekly where she hears the Word of God. Her children and other Christians talk about the Word of God at home. Someone in the home always reads the Bible every day for family worship. She is also active as a woman leader of the church and frequently witnesses to others about her faith in Christ. She has found real strength in the Christian women who have formed a team to work together in different gardens. After cultivation they eat the food they have brought and prepared. They sing hymns while they cultivate and pray afterwards. Sometimes the Bible is also read. Other non-Christian teams have formed which sing worldly songs. This group is an alternative for Christians. As these Christians work together, sing together, pray together, listen to the Word of God together, their faith grows.

Mary never feels the need to return to the ancestors. Christ is all she needs, according to her own words. When asked what can be done to help weaker Christians, her response is instruction from the Word of God. The team of women visits different homes, testifying and encouraging other women. Her area in Kitui has been reached with the Gospel. What is needed is restoration of the weak Christians, she believes.

Some African theologians advocate absorption of the ancestors into African Christianity much as the Roman Catholics have their cult of the dead saints (cf. Fashole-Luke 1974b). When she was asked about bringing the living-dead into Christianity, she spoke adamantly. These people are wrong, she said, for they are trying to mix things that do not mix. If Christ lives with in the heart, the ancestors cannot. If the ancestors are there, Christ cannot be. And these ancestors from Mary's perspective are the ancestors who were once living. Each medicine man has his own ancestral spirit who was formerly a medicine man himself. That ancestral spirit instructs and empowers the medicine man in his work. Therefore, the whole traditional practice of ancestral spirits and the medicine man must depart from the Christian's life.

How then should we honour our ancestors? Mary responds that the only way they were honoured in the past was by sacrifice and offerings. They were given their share of blood and meat. Can a Christian pour out libations in honour of his ancestors? Her reply was positively not. Pouring libations is tied to the old way of life. To do so is to drift backwards. It is not fitting for a Christian to give libations.

Here we find a strong, firm Christian testimony. It would be worthwhile relating the testimony of Musango, that elder who led her to the Lord. For he and his family were not always strong Christians.

Although Musango and his wife were professing Christians formerly, they were not strong in their faith. Only God knows whether they were born again. When trouble struck them they resorted to the medicine man who provided magical water to protect them from bewitching. But God was good to him in many ways, giving him a profitable business and a model son who was the envy of the village. This aroused jealousy from some. One day in early 1975, Musango's relative became drunk. In his drunken stupor he told Musango, "Your business will shut down and you will become like all the rest of us. Your son Jonathan will begin failing and failing in school until my son catches up to him and they will both study together in Secondary School."

With that word Musango's whole family was filled with fear. They knew they would be bewitched. True to his word, tragedy began to strike. Musango closed down his business and opened up a beer hall. But the men did not pay for their drinks and began stealing bottles. He himself began drinking, bringing havoc to the family with his drunken stupor. His son Jonathan became ill whenever he went to school and his marks began to plummet. Everyone knew that these troubles were due to the bewitching by their relatives.

Their 14 year old son Jonathan was a Sunday School teacher in the local A.I.C. church. During a Sunday School seminar conducted by the pastor, Jonathan realized for the first time that he was not a Christian, even though he had assumed he was because of being born in a Christian home. That day he placed his personal faith in Christ. After the seminar Jonathan shared with the pastor the problems in his family. Pastor David taught him that Bible verse, "Greater is He who is in you than he who is in the world." The pastor assured him that Christ was all powerful and there was nothing to fear.

With this new found faith he ran home to his mother with the good news of his faith in Christ. He also assured her that he had the answer for their family problems. They should remove all their fetishes and trust only the Lord. Because of their desperate straits they agreed, but thought they should call a medicine man to remove the charms. Jonathan assured them that this was not necessary. He would remove them with his own hands. One by one he extracted the charms from the places where the medicine man had placed them. This little boy of faith then began to lead the family into total trust in the Lord.

God remarkably heard. The son's illness left him immediately and his marks in school shot up. The father sold the beer hall and opened up his former business again. Peace was once more restored to the family. They began to enjoy prosperity again.

To this day some Christians ask the father, "Musango, what powerful witch doctor do you visit?" When he denies that he has any charms, they don't believe him. "Come," they say, "we know you have charms planted in your shop and running straight up the hill to your own pillow." They simply cannot believe that such peace and prosperity is possible by trusting God alone. Christians believe that Christ is not enough. They need Christ plus something else. When Jonathan was growing up, he knew the family claimed to be Christian. But they always seemed to need something more. Christ was not sufficient. Many Christians still believe that they need traditional protection from the ancestors in addition to their Christian faith (Musango 1983:P.I.).

God's people need to be taught the Word of God as it applies to the various needs of the African context. If African Christians are going to thrive as believers without resorting to the traditional religion, they shall need to be grounded in their faith. Biblical teaching is not indoctrination. What these people need is not more information. New facts even from the Bible are inadequate. They need to be taught by the Holy Spirit through God's servants who expound the Word of God, line upon line, precept upon precept. As the Word of God fills their minds and the Holy Spirit energizes His Word, God's people will be strengthened to stand against the wiles of the Devil.

Teaching may take many forms, but they are most effective when indigenous. Enacting the stories of the Bible through drama is helpful when an oral lesson is communicated. Drama is one medium that has not been developed sufficiently by the Christian Church. The moral lessons are not only learned by the youth who participate but by the older ones who may be illiterate. Telling biblical and moral stories by the elders to the youth is both entertaining and character building. Memorizing traditional proverbs or biblical proverbs which teach moral values should be pursued. Not only should they be learned in the schools which is done today, but also in the Christian homes. Singing traditional melodies with biblical quotations is an excellent method of hiding God's Word in the heart.

Biblical instruction rests on two pillars: the local church and the Christian home. The pastor must be trained in the Bible. This need not be in an institutional school but may be through extension or correspondence. The chief quality of the pastor is not the Bible School Diploma but an eager heart, faithfully studying the Scripture and growing as he learns. There are effective pastors who do not have formal Bible training. Conversely, there are many Bible School graduates whose hearts are not in the ministry of the Word of God and consequently they are ineffective. But there can be no effective pastor anywhere who is not born again by the Spirit of God, filled with the Spirit, and learning daily from the Word of God

113

so that he can minister to the people. The pastor must cooperate with active elders who are of the same quality as the pastor. As the pastor and elders teach the Word of God from the pulpit, instruct new believers in catechism, oversee the children, youth and adults in their various services, and shepherd the flock in home visitation, the Christian believers will grow in their faith and be able to resist the wiles of the Devil.

The Christian home is indispensable. In many areas the Christian home is disintegrating with the father working elsewhere and the children attending boarding school. Here is an area that requires urgent attention if the Body of Christ is to flourish. The father must exercise the traditional role as leader in the nurture and discipline of the children. Christian parents cannot leave biblical instruction to the schools or the church. A Christian home without regular family worship is a weak home. A Christian home without the father and mother both active in leading their children to a personal faith in Christ, and teaching them the practical truths from the Word of God will inevitably be a weak home. The whole fabric of society disintegrates when the family relationships are not strong, built upon biblical principles.

Where there is vital, dynamic biblical instruction through the local church and the Christian home, there you may expect to find strong Christians. Wherever there is healthy body life within the Body of Christ, each Christian ministering and sharing with the others, there you will find less problems with the ancestral cult. Biblical instruction is from pulpit to pew, from parent to child, from one believer to another believer. It is both formal and informal, scheduled and impromptu. Effective instruction in the Word of God takes place when people are live Christians and functioning in the Body of Christ as God intended, according to His Word. "Faith cometh by hearing and hearing by the Word of God." And only through that kind of faith can the adversaries of God's Kingdom be defeated.

As evangelicals we must understand that the secret for a dynamic and effective, growing Christian Church anywhere is a living faith in Jesus Christ and a hunger for the Word of God. African Christian Theology will be nothing if it is not built on the Bible. And the Christian Church in Africa will be nothing unless it draws deeply from the wells of living water in the Scriptures.

### Africanized Theology- A Necessity for Evangelicals

Evangelicals are known as people of the Book. They are the ones who gave the Bible to the people in the first place. Prior to the Reformation the Bible could only be entrusted to the priests who were often illiterate anyway. But with the advent of the Reformation the great emphasis was giving the Bible to the people. It is a known historical fact that the rise of schools in the West was through the emphasis of the evangelicals wanting to help the believers to read and write so that they could have access to the Word of God. And in the same way the development of schools in Africa through the missions was for that same purpose- to help the Christians read their own Bibles.

114

# PERMISSION ACKNOWLEDGEMENTS

The author expresses his gratitude to those individuals and publishers listed below who have kindly granted permission to reproduce or utilize their materials in this book. Those shorter quotations which do not require formal permission are duly acknowledged within the text. The value of all those books and articles utilized in the production of this book are greatly appreciated and gratefully acknowledged by the author.

"The African Church Struggles into her Third Century" Tokunboh Adeyemo. **Christianity Today** XXIII (July), 14-17 (1040-1043), 1979.

**African Religions and Philosophy** John Mbiti.
Heinemann Educational Books Ltd. London, 1969.

**African Religions in Western Scholarship** Okot p'Bitek.
East African Literature Bureau, Nairobi, 1970.

**African Theology: Its Nature, Problems and Methods** Charles Nyamiti.
Gaba Publications, Eldoret, Kenya, 1971.

"African Theology: Origin, Methodology and Content" Kwesi Dickson.
**Journal of Religious Thought.** 32:34-45,1975.

**All Africa Lutheran Consultation on Christian Theology and Theological Education in the African Context: Background Materials I.** Geneva: Lutheran World Federation, Department of Church Cooperation, 1978.

"The Biblical Basis for Present Trends in African Theology" John Mbiti.
**African Theology En Route** K. Appiah-Kubi and S. Torres eds., pp. 83-94. Maryknoll, NY: Orbis Books, 1979.

"Christian Theology in Africa" Peter Kanyandago. **African Ecclesiastical Review** XX 3:339-348, 1979.

**Christianity in Independent Africa** E. Fashole-Luke, R. Gray and A. Hastings eds. Indiana University Press, Bloomington, Illinois. Permission applied for.

**Contextualization: A Theology of Gospel and Culture** Bruce Nicholls.
InterVarsity Press, Downers Grover, Illinois, 1979.

**Crucial Issues in Missions Tomorrow** Donald McGavran ed. Chicago: The Moody Bible Institute of Chicago, 1972.

Davis, Linnell. Missionary with the Africa Inland Mission.

**Evangelical Review of Theology** New Delhi: World Evangelical Fellowship Theological Commission. VII 1, 1983.

Jonathan Musango. Pastor of the Africa Inland Church, Kitui, Kenya.

Muema Joel. Pastor of the Africa Inland Church, Kitui, Kenya.

Nairobi Evangelical Graduate School of Theology, Nairobi, Kenya.

**New Testament Christianity for Africa and the World** M. Glasswell and E. Fashole-Luke eds. London: SPCK, 1974.

**New Testament Eschatology in an African Background** John Mbiti. London: Oxford University Press, 1971.

"Recent Studies of African Religions" Benjamin Ray. **History of Religions** XII (Aug.): 75-89, 1972.

"Theological Impotence and the Universality of the Church". John Mbiti. **Lutheran World** XXI 3:251-260, 1974.

**Theological Pitfalls in Africa** Byang Kato. Nairobi: Evangel Publishing House, 1975.

"Time in Traditional African Thought" John Parratt. **Religion** VII:117-126, 1977.

**White Man's Country: Lord Delamere and the Making of Kenya** Elspeth Huxley. London: Chatto & Windus, 1970.

118

# BIBLIOGRAPHY OF REFERENCES CITED

## Includes Bibliography of African Christian Theology

Following are the abbreviations used in the text referring to various documents cited in the following bibliography.

| | |
|---|---|
| A.I.C. | Africa Inland Church |
| A.I.M. | Africa Inland Mission |
| A.M.S. | Alliance of Mission Societies |
| C.C.K.C. | Continuation Committee of Kikuyu Conference |
| C.K.E. | Conference of Kikuyu Elders |
| C.S. | Church of Scotland |
| H.D | Hearing and Doing (early A.I.M. periodical) |
| K.M.C. | Kenya Missionary Council |
| P.I. | Personal Interview |
| T.I. | Taped Interview |
| U.M.S. | United Missionary Society, Kikuyu |

Adeyemo, Tokumboh
1979a    **Salvation in African Tradition**. Nairobi: Evangel Publishing House.

1979b    "The African Church Struggles into her Third Century." **Christianity Today.** XXIII (July), 14-17 (1040-1043).

1983    "Towards an Evangelical African Theology." **Evangelical Review of Theology.** VII, 1:147-154.

Agbeti, J.
1972    "African Theology: What it is?" **Presence.** pp.7ff

Alliance of Mission Societies, Kenya
1922    Minutes of the Representative Council of the Alliance of Missionary Societies in Kenya Colony, Aug. 31 - Sept. 2, 1922. Archives of the National Christian Council of Kenya, Nairobi.

Anderson, Gerald H. and Thomas F. Stransky eds.
1976    **Mission Trends No. 3. Third World Theologies.** Grand Rapids: Wm. B. Eerdmans Pub. Co.

Anderson, J.N.D.
1970    **Christianity and Comparative Religion.** London: Tyndale Press.

Andersson, Efraim
1968    **Churches At The Grass Roots.** N.Y.: Friendship Press

Appiah-Kubi, Kofi
1979    **African Theology En Route.** Maryknoll, N.Y.: Orbis Books.

Arthur, John W.
  n.d.          Letter to Bishop Peel, 21st Sept. 15 [sic]
                Archives of the Africa Inland Mission, International,
                Nairobi.

Association of Third World Theologians.
  1978          "Pan African Conference of Third World Theologians
                Communique." **IDOC Bulletin.** 1 (Jan. 1978), pp. 3-6.

Baeta C.G.
  1964          "The Younger Churches: An African Viewpoint." **Religion
                in Life.** 34 (Winter 1964-1965), pp. 15-24.

Bares, A.
  1978a         **All Africa Lutheran Consultation on Christian Theology
                and Theological Education in the African Context:
                Background Materials I.** Geneva.

  1978b         **All Africa Lutheran Consultation on Christian Theology
                and Theological Education in the African Context:
                Background Materials II.** Geneva.

Barlow, A Ruffell
  1925          "Report and Recommendations Regarding Possibilities of
                Uniformity in Church Discipline in the Native Churches of
                the Alliance." Prepared for the Alliance of Missionary
                Societies, August 1925. Archives of the National Christian
                Council of Kenya, Nairobi.

Barnett, Eric
  1982          A.I.M. missionary, second generation. Personal Interview.

Barrett, David B.
  1968          **Schism and Renewal in Africa.** London: Oxford University
                Press.

  1973          **Kenya Churches Handbook.** Kisumu, Kenya: Evangel
                Publishing House.

  1982          **World Christian Encylopedia.** Nairobi: Oxford University
                Press.

Baxter, Jean
  1982          A.I.M. missionary, Kapsabet, Nandi. Personal Interview.

Becken, Hand-Jurgen ed.
  1972          **Relevant Theology for Africa.** Durban: Lutheran House.

Booth, Newell S.
  1975          "Time and Change in African Traditional Thought."
                **Journal of Religion in Africa.** VII, 2, pp. 81-91.

Bowers, Paul
  1980          "Evangelical Theology in Africa: Byang Kato's Legacy."
                **Trinity Journal.** I (Spring), pp. 84-87.

Bryson, Stuart M.
1959    **Light in Darkness: The Story of the Nandi Bible.** London: Parry Jackman Scripture Illustrations Ltd., 1959.

Buswell III, James Oliver
1978a    "Contextualization: Is it only a New Word for Indigenization?" **Evangelical Missions Quarterly.** XIV: 13-20.

1978b    "Contextualization: Theory, Tradition and Method." **Theology and Mission.** David Hesselgrave ed., pp. 87-111. Grand Rapids: Baker Book House.

Buthelezi, Manas
1973a    "An African Theology or a Black Theology." **Black Theology: The South African Voice.** B. Moore ed. London: Hurst.

1973b    "African Theology and Black Theology: A Search for a Theological Method." **Relevant Theology for Africa.** H.J. Becken ed. Durban.

Cagnolo, C.
1933    **The Akikuyu.** Nyeri, Kenya: Mission Printing School.

Christian Council of the Gold Coast
1955    **Christianity and African Culture.** Accra: Christian Council of the Gold Coast.

Church of Scotland
1926    "African Church Laws, As Revised." Archives of National Christian Council of Kenya, Nairobi.

Coe, Shoki and Aharon Sapsezian
1972    **Ministry in Context.** Theological Education Fund.

Cole, E.K.
1957    **A History of Church Co-Operation in Kenya.** Limuru, Kenya: St. Paul's College Press.

Cone, James H.
1970    **A Black Theology of Liberation.** Philadelphia: J.B. Lippincott Co.

Conference of Kikuyu Elders
1929    Minutes of a Conference of Kikuyu Church Elders, March 8-12. Archives of the National Christian Council of Kenya, Nairobi.

Continuation Committee of Kikuyu Conference
1918    Minutes of the Continuation Committee of Kikuyu Conference, Ap. 29, 1918. Archives of the National Christian Council of Kenya, Nairobi.

Cope, T.H.
1979    **The Africa Inland Mission in Kenya - Aspects of its History (1895-1945).** M.Phil. Dissertation, London University.

Covell, Ralph
    1977      Book Review of "Waterbuffalo Theology" by Kasuke Koyama. **Evangelical Missions Quarterly,** Jan. 1977, pp. 55, 56.

Cullmann, Oscar
    1964      **Christ and Time.** Floyd V. Filson transl., Philadelphia: The Westminster Press.

Daidanso, Djongwe
    1983      "An African Critique of African Theology." **Evangelical Review of Theology.** VII, 1:63-72

Davis, Linnell E. and Martha
    1982      A.I.M. missionaries, second generation, Machakos. Personal Interview.

Dickson, Kwesi
    1973      "The Old Testament and African Theology." **Ghana Bulletin of Theology** 4:31-41.

    1974      "Towards a Theologia Africana." **New Testament Christianity for Africa and the World.** M. Glasswell and E. Fashole-Luke eds., pp. 198-207. London.

    1975      "African Theology: Origin, Methodology and Content." **Journal of Religious Thought.** 32:34-45.

Dickson, Kwesi and Paul Ellingworth
    1969      **Biblical Revelation and African Beliefs.** London: Lutterworth Press.

Fashole-Luke, Edward W.
    1974a      "What is African Christian Theology? **Communio Viatorum.** 17:97-102.

    1974b      "Ancestor Veneration and the Communion of Saints." **New Testament Christianity for Africa and the World.** Mark Glasswell and Edward Fashole-Luke eds. London: SPCK.

    1981      "Footpaths and Sign Posts to African Christian Theologies." **Scottish Journal of Theology.** 34 No. 5, 19-40, Ja-Je 81.

Fleming, Bruce
    1980      **Contextualization of Theology.** Pasadena: William Carey Library.

Gaussen, L.
    n.d.      **The Plenary Inspiration of the Holy Scriptures.** Chicago: The Bible Institute Colportage Ass'n.

Gelzer, David G.
    1970      "Random Notes on Black Theology and African Theology." **Christian Century. XVI:1091-1093.**

Glasswell, M.E.
    1975    "Can there be an African or a Black Theology?" **The Modern Churchman.** XVIII, 4:164-172.

Glasswell, Mark and Edward W. Fashole-Luke.
    1974    **New Testament Christianity for Africa and the World: Essays in Honour of Henry Sawyer.** London: SPCK.

Goba, Bonganjalo
    1979    "An African Christian Theology." **Journal of Theology for Southern Africa.** XXVI:3-12.

Goreham, N.J.
    1975    "Towards an African Theology." **The Expository Times.** 86:233-36.

Gration, John A.
    1974    **The Relationship of the A.I.M. and its National Church in Kenya Between 1895 and 1971.** Ph. D. Dissertation, New York University.

Guilding, Mr. and Mrs. W.J.
    n.d.    A.I.M. missionary and first Principal of Ukamba Bible Institute. Taped Interview by Linnell Davis.

Harjula, Raimo
    1970    "Towards a Theologia Africana." **Student Essays and Religious Workshop Papers.** Limuru.

Hassing, Per
    1971    "Christian Theology in Africa." **Religion in Life.** 40:510-518.

**Hearing and Doing**
            Vols. I-XXI, 1898-1916. Mission periodical of Africa Inland Mission.

Henry, Carl F.H. ed.
    1958    **Revelation and the Bible.** Philadelphia, PA: Presbyterian and Reformed Publishing Co.

Huxley, Elspeth
    1970    **White Man's Country: Lord Delamere and the Making of Kenya.** Vol. I. London: Chatto & Windus (first printed 1935).

Idowu, E. Bolaji
    1973    **African Traditional Religion: A Definition.** Maryknoll, N.Y.: Orbis Books.

Imasogie, Osadolor
    1973    **Guidelines for Christian Theology in Africa.** Ghana: African Christian Press.

123

Jacobs, Donald R.
1966    **Christian Theology in Africa.** Mt. Joy, Pennsylvania; mimeographed.

Kanyandago, Peter
1978    "Christian Theology in Africa." **African Ecclesiastical Review.** XX, 3:339-348.

Kato, Byang H.
1975    **Theological Pitfalls in Africa.** Kisumu, Kenya: Evangel Publishing House.
1976    "Theological Issues in Africa." **Bibliotheca Sacra.** 133:143-152.
1985    **Biblical Christianity in Africa.** Ghana: African Christian Press.

Kenya Missionary Council
1927    Minutes of the Annual General Meeting of the Kenya Missionary Council, 1927. Archives of the National Christian Council of Kenya, Nairobi.
1930    Minutes of the Annual General Meeting of The Kenya Missionary Council, 1930. Archives of the National Christian Council of Kenya. Nairobi.

Kinney, John W.
1979    "The Theology of John Mbiti: His Sources, Norms, and Methods." **Occasional Bulletin.** III, 2:65-67.

Koyama, Kosuke
1976    **Waterbuffalo Theology.** Maryknoll, NY. Orbis Books

Kraemer, Hendrik
1963    **The Christian Message in a Non-Christian World.** Grand Rapids: Kregel Pub.

Kurewa, J.W. Zvumunondita
1975    "The Meaning of African Theology." **Journal of Theology for Southern Africa.** II:34-42.

Lausanne Committee for World Evangelization
1978    **The Willowbank Report- Gospel and Culture.** Wheaton, Illinois: Lausanne Committee for World Evangelization.

Leakey, L.S.B.
1952    **Mau Mau and the Kikuyu.** London.

Long, Charles H.
1975    "Structural Similarities and Dissimilarities in Black and African Theologies." **Journal of Religious Thought.** 32:9-24.

Lugira, A.M.
1979    "African Christian Theology." **African Theological Journal.** VIII:50-61.

Lundblad, Janet

    1978      "Towards an Authentic African Theology." **Covenant Quarterly.** 36:37-47.

Mary

    1983      A.I.C. Christian, Kyamatu, Kitui. Personal Interview

Mbiti, John S.

    1966      **Akamba Stories.** London.

    1969      **African Religions and Philosophy.** London: SPCK.

    1970a    "The Future of Christianity in Africa." **Communio Viatorum** XIII, 1-2:32-33.

    1970b    "Sources for the Study of African Traditional Religion." **Student Essays and Religious Workshop Papers,** Limuru, Kenya.

    1970c    **Concepts of God in Africa.** London: SPCK.

    1971      **New Testament Eschatology in an African Background.** London: Oxford University Press.

    1972a    "Christianity and Traditional Religion in Africa." **Crucial Issues in Missions Tomorrow.** Donald MacGavran ed. Chicago: Moody Press.

    1972b    "The Growing Respectability of African Traditional Religion." **Lutheran World** IX, 1:54-58

    1973      "African Theology." **Worldview.** XVI:33-39.

    1974a    "Theological Impotence and the Universality of the Church." **Lutheran World.** XXI, 3:251-260.

    1975a    **An Introduction to African Religion.** London: London University Press.

    1975b    **The Prayers of African Religion.** N.Y.: Orbis Books.

    1976      "The Theology of the New World. I. Some Current Concerns of African Theology." Expository Times. 87:164-168.

    1978a    "Theology of the New World. Some Current Concerns of African Theology." **Expository Times.** 87:164-168.

    1978b    "African Theology." **All African Lutheran Consultation on Theology in the African Context: Background Material I.,** pp. 33-38. Geneva.

    1979      "The Biblical Basis for Present Trends in African Theology." **African Theology En Route.** K. Appiah-Kubi and S. Torres eds., pp. 83-94. Maryknoll, N.Y.: Orbis Books, 1979.

1986    **Bible and Theology in African Community.** Nairobi Oxford University Press, 1986.

Miller, Catherine S.

n.d.    **Peter Cameron Scott.** London: Parry Jackman

Mshana, E.E.

1972    "The Challenges of Black and African Theology." **Presence** V:2-4.

Muema, Joel

Mukamba Christian, pastor in the A.I.C. and former student at Scott Theological College, Machakos, Kenya.

Muga, Erasto

1975    **African Response to Western Christian Religion.** Nairobi: East African Literature Bureau.

Murray-Brown, Jeremy

1972    **Kenyatta** London: George Allen & Unwin Ltd.

Musango, Jonathan

A.I.C. pastor in Kitui. Personal Interview.

McGavran, Donald ed.

1972    **Crucial Issues in Missions Tomorrow.** Chicago: Moody Press.

McVeigh, Malcolm J. "Sources for An African Christian Theology." **Presence.** V, 3:2,3.

Nichols, Bruce

1979a    **Contextualization: A Theology of Gospel and Culture.** Illinois: Inter Varsity Press.

1979b    "Towards a Theology of Gospel and Culture." **Gospel and Culture.** John Stott and Robert Coote eds., pp. 69-82. Pasadena: Wm. Carey Library.

1983    **Evangelical Review of Theology.** VII, 1.

Nixon, Harmon

1940    Letter to Ralph Davis, Sept. 6, 1940. File 14, Box 23, Collection 81, Archives of the Billy Graham Center, Wheaton, Illinois.

Nyamiti, Charles

1971    **African Theology: Its Nature, Problems and Methods.** Kampala: Gaba Publications.

1973    **The Scope of African Theology.** Kampala: Gaba Publications.

Okeke, George K.
    1978    "Indigenization of Christianity in Africa." **Communio Viatorum.** XXI:49-57.

Oliver, Roland
    1966    **The Missionary Factor in East Africa.** London: Longmans, Green And Co.

Padilla, C. Rene
    1979    "Hermeneutics and Culture- An Anthropological Perspective." **Gospel and Culture.** John Stott and Robert Coote eds., pp. 83-108. Pasadena: Wm. Carey Library.

Pan African Conference of Third World Theologians
    1978    "Communique." **IDOC Bulletin.** No. 1 (Jan.), 3-6.

Parratt, John
    1977    "Time in Traditional African Thought." **Religion.** VII-117-126.

P'Bitek, Okot
    1970    **African Religions in Western Scholarship.** Nairobi: East African Literature Bureau.

Peterson, Dean A.
    1970    "A Summary Report on the 1969 African Theological Faculty Conference." **Lutheran World.** XVII, 1:65-69.

Pobee, John S.
    1979    **Towards an African Theology.** Nashville, Tenn.: The Parthenon Press.

Ray, Benjamin
    1972a   "Book Reviews: Recent Studies of African Religions." **History of Religions.** XII (Aug.) :75-89.

Roberts, J.D.
    1978-79 "Black Theology and African Theology." **INS** 3:14-27.

Rubingh, Eugene
    1972    "The African Shape of the Gospel." **His.** XXXIII, 2:9-11.

Sandgren, David P.
    1976    **The Kikuyu, Christianity, and the Africa Inland Mission.** Ph.D. Dissertation, Unversity of Wisconsin.

Sawyerr, Harry
    1963    "The Basis of a Theology for Africa." **International Review of Mission.** LII:266-278.
    1971    "What is African Theology?" **African Theological Journal.** No. 4, Aug., 7-24.

Schopp, Ludwig ed.
    1947    **The Fathers of the Church: The Apostolic Fathers.** Francis Glimm, Joseph Marique and Gerald Walsh transls. N.Y.: Cima Pub. Co., Inc.

Setiloane, Gabrial
1980     "Theological Trends in Africa." **Missionalia** 8, 47-53,
         Aug. 80.

Seoul Declaration
1983     "The Seoul Declaration Toward an Evangelical Theology
         for the Third World." **Evangelical Review of Theology.**
         VII, 1:8-12

Shorter, Aylward
1975     **African Christian Theology - Adaptation or Incarnation.**
         London: Geoffrey Chapman Press.

Stauffacher, John
1927a    Letter to H.D. Campbell, Jan. 17, 1927. File 10,

         Box 13, Collection 81. Archives of the Billy Graham
         Center, Wheaton, Illinois.
1927b    Letter to H. D. Campbell, Feb. 23, 1927. File 10,

         Box 13, Collection 81. Archives of the Billy Graham
         Center, Wheaton, Illinois.
1929     Letter to H.D. Campbell, Nov. 19, 1929. File 10,

         Box 13, Collection 81. Archives of Billy Graham Center,
         Wheaton, Illnois.
1930a    Letter to H.D. Campbell, Feb. 11, 1930. File 10,

         Box 13, Collection 81. Archives of the Billy Graham
         Center Wheaton, Illinois.
1930b    Letter to H.D. Campbell, Ap 23, 1930. File 10,

         Box 13, Collection 81. Archives of the Billy Graham
         Center, Wheaton, Illinois.
1930c    Letter to H.D. Campbell, Sept. 17, 1930. File 10,

         Box 13, Collection 81. Archives of the Billy Graham
         Center,Wheaton, Illinois.

Stott, John and Robert Coote eds.

1979     **Gospel and Culture.** Wm. Carey Library.

Stumpf, Hulda
1927     Letter to Campbell, May 3, 1927. File 24, Box 24, Collection
         81. Archives of the Billy Graham Center, Wheaton, Illinois.

Sundkler, Bengt Gustav
1960     "Towards Christian Theology in Africa." **The Christian
         Ministry in Africa.,** pp. 281-317. London: SMC

Taber, Charles R.
1979     "Hermeneutics and Culture - An Anthropological
         Perspective." **Gospel and Culture.** John Stott and Robert
         Coote eds. Wm. Pasadena: Wm. Carey Library.

Tenney, Merrill C. ed.
1960 **The Word For This Century.** N.Y.: Oxford University Press.

Thomas, J.C.
1973 "What is African Theology? **Ghana Bulletin of Theology.** IV, 4:14-30.

Tienou, Tite
1982 **The Theological Task of the Church in Africa.** Ghana: African Christian Press, 1982.
1983 "Biblical Foundations: An African Study." **Evangelical Review of Theology.** VII, 1:89-101.

Torres, Sergio and Virginia Fabella
1978 **The Emergent Gospel.** Maryknoll, N.Y.: Orbis Books.

Tutu, Desmond M.
1975 "Black Theology/African Theology- Soul Mates or Antagonists?" **Journal of Religious Thought.** XXXII:25-33.
1978 "Whither African Theology?" **Christianity in Independent Africa.** E. Fashole-Luke, R. Gray and A. Hastings eds. Bloomington: Indiana University Press.

Ukpong, Justin S.
1984 **African Theologies Now - A Profile.** Eldoret, Kenya: Gaba Publications.

United Missionary Society, Kikuyu
1913 Minutes of the United Missionary Conference, Kikuyu, June 17-22, 1913. Archives of the National Christian Council of Kenya, Nairobi.

Uzukwu, Eugene
1977 "Notes on Methodology for an African Theology." **African Ecclesiastical Review** XIX, 3:155-164.

Wright, G. Ernest
1953 **The Old Testament Against Its Environment.** London: SCM Press.

Wenham, J.W.
1955 **Our Lord's View of the Old Testament.** London: The Tyndale Press.

Yamaori, Tsunao
1975 **Christopaganism or Indigenous Christianity?** Pasadena: Wm. Carey Library.

# THE AUTHOR

Rev. Dr. Richard J. Gehman was born in Norristown, Pennsylvania, U.S.A., December 24, 1935. He earned a B.A. in Anthropology in 1960 from Wheaton College, Wheaton, Illinois; an M.A. in New Testament from Wheaton College Graduate School; an M.Div. in 1963 from Gordon Divinity School, Wenham, Massachusetts; and a Doctor of Missiology in 1985 from the School of World Mission of Fuller Theological Seminary, Pasadena, California.

Born in a Christian home, the son of a pastor, he was taught from earliest years of the need for conversion and a personal faith in Jesus Christ. At the age of five he was born again through repentance and faith in Christ. Later he was baptized and became a member of the Mennonite Brethren in Christ Church.

From 1963 to 1966 he taught in Berean Bible School in Allentown, Pennsylvania, from which he had graduated earlier in 1957 with a Diploma in Theology. In 1971 he was ordained to the Christian ministry by the Bible Fellowship Church in which denomination he served as pastor for one year.

Since 1966 he together with his wife, Florence, have been serving with the Africa Inland Mission in Kenya, East Africa, at Scott Theological College. For eight years he served as Principal of the College, during which time the College was fully accredited by the Accrediting Council for Theological Education in Africa (ACTEA) and the Bachelor of Theology Degree programme was launched. In 1983 he handed the leadership of the college over to a Kenyan.

For two years since 1985 he has assisted in the pastoral ministry of a particular church in Nairobi of the Africa Inland Church. He is also facilitating the development of theological reflection among the churches in eastern Africa. And he has served as a member of the Board of Governors for the Evangelical Graduate School of Theology (NEGST) in Nairobi from its very inception.

He is married to Florence A. Hilbert. They have two children, Nathan Scott and Joy Elizabeth.